Behind The Scenes

JANICE F. PRYOR

Dedication

This book is dedicated to my awesome children, Avies, Robert Jr, Monique, Mike, Edell, Eddie, and Charles may he rest in peace,

A special dedication also to my beloved aunt Lois Reid may she rest in peace.

And to God who has kept me, provided for me, protected me and saved me while equipping me with his gifts.

Acknowledgements

Team work makes the dream work and with my team, I had full support while working on this project. A special thank you to all of you.

1. To my mentor Karen Curry a published author who spent many hours walking me through the process and keeping me on track

2. To my cousin Joycettee who stepped in and spent many hours editing the book and providing inspiring suggestions

3. To my sister and brother-in-Law, Martha and James Gills for supporting me in this project and providing excellent feedback which really encouraged me to keep going

4. To my family who was there for me with suggestions, brainstorming, by coming up with ideas and selecting pictures for the book cover

5. To my good friend Lonnell Poole who was my support by reading, reviewing photos, cover designs, making recommendations, providing sound advise and encouraged me through this process.

6. Most of all to God who loved us so much that he gave his only begotten Son.

CONTENTS

Introduction

I am a country girl, born and raised in Goldsboro, North Carolina. Our lives consisted of living in low-income housing after moving from Faro, North Carolina to Goldsboro, North Carolina. I was the kid that spent her lunch money on those delicious scalloped butter cookies on the way to school and would cry my eyeballs out at lunch time because I had no money to buy my lunch.

I remember being dragged on the cotton sack because everyone had to be in the cotton field at a certain time, and there was no such thing as a babysitter. Because times were hard, I learned how to work in the fields putting in tobacco, picking peppers, and learning to preserve food for the winter.

Suddenly, my mother moved to Chicago Heights, Illinois to find a better life for us. After a short while, she sent for us to move to Chicago as well. After our arrival all I heard from my mom was do not go up there on

Wentworth Avenue in Chicago Heights. Many things were happening up there on Wentworth; drinking, partying, and hanging out on the corner.

As soon as we arrived in Chicago Heights Illinois, we had our first foot long hotdog. Yep, you guessed right. I went to find out where Wentworth Avenue was. You are right again; this was no place for a country girl who just landed in the city and definitely wasn't street smart.

CHAPTER 1

Train Up A Child

L iving in the country as a kid was a lot of fun. We would take the silver spoons, knives, and forks outside and play in the dirt with them all day if we wanted to. It was always nice sitting under the fruit trees getting shade from the sun. After our play time was over, Mother Pearlie had the shiniest silver in Faro, North Carolina. Every day, my grandfather and all the family members old enough to work went to the fields to work the tobacco.

One day, they were gone and my cousin Daron played on the porch, so I thought I would give him a haircut. I ran into the house and got the scissors and cut his hair. He was cooperative and didn't give me much fuss about it. After I finished this once in a lifetime haircut, I put the scissors away and we played until everyone returned home from the field.

Well, after everyone was home, Aunt Pearlina noticed there was a big plug of hair missing out of Daron's head and the first person they turned to was me. Needless to say, I never tried to cut anyone's hair again.

We didn't have any bathrooms in the house. We had to use slop jars for the bathroom which was kept in your room until it was time to empty it and clean it. There were no closets either. The clothes hung in the corner of the room and a sheet was draped across the clothes to hide them. I can't remember how many people shared a room, but I know we were piled up like sardines in one room. With no bathtub, we had to wash up every night in the wash basin to ensure we stayed clean.

One day a lot of commotion was going on outside and everybody was screaming. Good Lord, the sow got out of the hog pen and Daddy Will was chasing the hog around the house trying to catch her. He ran so long trying to catch that hog, he almost passed out. Mother Pearlie was in the kitchen trying to fix supper and dropped everything to see about Daddy Will. Eventually, they calmed him down and got him in the house.

Meanwhile, I was a happy camper because I was waiting on those good ole biscuits I loved so much. After summer was almost over and the tobacco was cured in the barn, it was time to prepare the tobacco for the market. At night, they would bring a truck load of tobacco and dump it on the porch then dragged into the house. Everyone would sit around the pot belly stove that had sweet potatoes on it and tie up the tobacco.

You had to grab a hand full of tobacco in your hand and make sure the ends were nice, even and neat. Then, you had to take one leaf of tobacco and fold it the length of the leaf just so, then wrap that one leaf around the top portion of the tobacco bundle. Tie it up real tight and put it to the side. No one stopped working until all the tobacco was wrapped up. Sometimes, we had a few workers that would roll up a few cigars while going through the process.

It looked like everyone was having a good time laughing from the joking and talking about what happened that day in the barn. I was sitting around waiting on the sweet potatoes to get done myself, I was too small to do anything else. I couldn't have been no older than four or five years old.

Sometimes Mother Pearlie would send us to go fetch the milk from down the road. Every time we had to go get the fresh milk, we had to pass by the cows. Those were the biggest cows I had ever seen in my life. It appeared they watched you all the way down the road. I kept my eyeballs on them as well, in case I needed to make a mad dash back to Mother Pearlie's house.

However, we got the milk back home safely and Mother Pearlie would get that good ole butter made by skimming the cream off the top of the milk. It seemed like cakes and pies lasted forever. They would bake cakes for the holiday and put them in the trunk and those were the best cakes and pies ever. The food lasted a long time back in the day.

It seemed like suddenly, I heard we are moving to Goldsboro, North Carolina. We were moving from the country to the city. We moved to Slaughter Street in the big pink house, right across the street from the church. The house had a big porch and when you walked into the house to the left was the living room and directly to the right was a bedroom. Behind the bedroom was a kitchen and down the hall were the stairs to the upper level where there were additional bedrooms. The bathroom was outside on the back porch. I wasn't too keen on the bathroom being on the back porch, but it was better than a slop jar. I always felt like I would fall in the slop jar.

Now that we were in the big city of Goldsboro, my Aunt Pearlina was going to night school to finish her high school degree and the kids did what kids do. We played all day and stayed away from the grown folk. My favorite place was under the house where I played with bugs. When you picked them up, they rolled up in a ball. I always enjoyed playing hopscotch, jack rocks, red light green light, Simon says, shooting marbles, and playing with my rick rack or you may know it as a paddle ball. Yep, that was the life.

On Saturdays, we had to get everything ready to go to church on Sunday. We had to polish our patent leather shoes with a biscuit, and get our cloths laid out for Sunday. I can't forget getting our hair done. My mother would wash, press, and curl my hair on Saturday, and I never liked the process. She would put alcohol in a tin can and set it on fire, put the pressing comb on the flame and press my hair until it was bone straight. Most of the time the hot grease would run down on my scalp and fry my brains out or at least it felt like that was what was happening. She would use so much grease to prevent my hair from sweating out or returning to being natural.

We had attended church in Faro, but since we lived across the street from a church, we often attended Sunday School there. On occasions, Mother Pearlie would attend Quarterly Meetings and they would have a good ole time service and wash feet. I didn't understand what was going on. My thought process was why didn't y'all wash your feet at home. Why bring your dirty feet to the church house? Now I know better. This act is an example of Christ manifesting his love for the disciples and our Lord humbled himself to serve his servants.

I remember one day some fishermen returned home from a successful fishing trip and they had a bucket full of catfish. I wanted some of that catfish because I loved seafood. However, Mother Pearlie said that catfish were scavengers at the bottom of the water and ate everything dead on the bottom. They had no scales on them with whiskers and we couldn't eat them. So, the only fish we could eat were Spots, which were actually a great pan fish.

As a child growing up I enjoyed dancing and wanted to take tap dancing, but my Grandmother said "it was a sin to dance" so that killed my dreams of tap dancing. However, I still danced every chance I got. Growing up in that house was truly a challenge as a kid. I guess it was because we moved from the country to the big city. We had neighbors right next door now and not up the road. I had to go to East End Elementary School, which I walked to. I had no problems while attending East End Elementary School.

One morning I was getting ready for school and Daron was awake. The tenants who worked at the bar-b-que house had left some fried chicken on the floor and Daron wanted some. Before leaving the house for school I instructed Daron not to eat the food because it had poison in it. I just said that because the food was left out over night and I didn't want him to eat it. I went to school and while at school. My grandmother, Mother Pearlie, noticed the children were acting strange. It turned out that they had eaten the food with the poison in it.

After I returned from school they were in the process of trying to see if Daron had eaten any of the food. Daron constantly said no he didn't eat any. My mother sent me to the store to buy a drank (Coke Cola). After I returned with the drank Daron asked if he could have some and they gave him a swallow. When Daron took a swallow, he immediately fell backwards, his eyes had rolled up in his head and looked like he was about to die that very moment. They knew then Daron had been poisoned as well. My mother ran for help and got a cab to take Daron to the hospital and they were able to save his life.

While living on Slaughter Street our cousins who were the tenants added additional people in the house. My mother then thought it was time for us to move. So, we did.

We moved to the projects, and we didn't have to worry about being too crowded in the house. One day, a friend from school came over to play on the merry go-round in our back yard. This friend dipped snuff. Out of the blue she asked me if I wanted to try and dip some snuff. I looked at her reluctantly and said I have never dipped snuff before. Still, she kept on bugging me and I eventually asked her to give me a pinch of it so I can taste it first.

I put it in my mouth and it was the nastiest and horrible taste I had ever tasted. Now mind you, she didn't tell me what to do with it, so I swallowed it. After a few turns on the merry go-round I was high as a kite with my head spinning. I felt like I needed to throw up. All I wanted to do was go home and lay down to sleep this snuff drunk away. I never ever dipped snuff again in my entire life.

While we were living in the projects, maintenance cut the grass, painted the apartments once a year and put horse manure around the trees to make them grow all nice and pretty. Although, immediately afterwards we had to hold our nose from the smell. The floors in the projects had this miracle wax on them, and we kept our floors shiny by putting on a pair of socks and sliding up and down the hallway after Mom would scrub the floors.

We didn't live too far from the school, so I didn't have much of a walk. My Mother's sister lived in Washington, DC and one summer Aunt Melothy and my cousin, Joycettee, paid us a visit. When the neighbors saw me and Joycettee together they thought we were twins. So, we played along for a while having people thinking we were twins.

We probably looked alike because her mother and my mother were sisters and her father and my father were first cousins. Another summer, my mother took a trip to Washington, DC. When she returned home, she was excited about this new record she heard while she was there. The record was called Green Onions and that was my first love of jazz music.

Growing up my sisters and I never had to go to the doctor to get our vaccinations, because the nurse came to the school. I remember her name to this day. Her name was Nurse Sikes. It should have been Nurse Yikes. You could tell she was in the school from the smell of alcohol when you entered the school. She had on a white uniform, white hosiery, white shoes and a white hat on her head with a bunch of needles. Every kid attending school that day had to get their shots, plus the booster shot that left a nice scar when it healed on your arm.

This was evidence that you received the booster shot. On shot day, they drew blood as well and that's when I learned I had a rare blood type of B negative. Today, AB negative is rarer than B negative, but back then

B Negative was the rarest blood type. They scared me when they realized I had the rare blood type and told me I had to get a list of people I knew with the same blood type as me. They told me I had to carry a card around with my blood type on it and as a matter of fact, they made me a card to keep on me the same day. I wanted to tell them "I'm only a kid and I don't know what you are talking about or what you mean. Please tell my momma for goodness sake." So, most of my life I felt like I needed to hold on to my blood because I wasn't going to be blood sisters with anyone.

My mom moved around a lot. She worked for the State hospital called Cherry Hospital and she only got paid once a month. Therefore, from the age of nine years old I had a big responsibility of watching my sisters. I had to get them ready for school, cook their food, wash their clothes, and entertain them. Sometimes when my mom got off work at 11pm, I would have her dinner done for her as well. I was going to school myself and sometimes I was late to school from trying to get my sisters ready first.

Most times, this got me in trouble and back then the teachers could paddle you behind the coat rack. When I was attending East End Elementary School, I had to go back to school one evening to discuss my project and my mom wasn't at home and couldn't take me back to school. I knew I wasn't supposed to leave the house, but I had to be at school for my project. I thought I could run to the school do my project and be back home before my mom got home. I always told my sisters that our light fixture had a camera and mom could see everything they were doing. So, I asked my little sisters to stay in the house and not to open the door.

I quickly dashed to the school to present my project, and it took longer than I thought. I was almost the last kid called to discuss my project, it was late and afterwards I had to walk back home. It was pitch black outside and I couldn't see anything. I'm sure the teachers didn't realize I was by myself that night or they would have given me a ride home. We lived on a dark street and you couldn't see anything except shadows. I was afraid to walk home straight down our street since I could see nothing. It felt like my tongue was in my throat. My heart was beating fast and my feet were moving as fast as they could.

I took the long way around on the main street which had streetlights. I was looking over my shoulders, afraid of my own shadow. I eventually got closer to home and cut through the neighbor's yard to get home safely. When I got home, oh my goodness, my mother was already there. When she got home, my sisters had opened the door and were laying in the door crying. The neighbors called her and told her what was going on. I couldn't say anything except I needed to be at school and just went to explain my project and was coming back home right afterwards. I am thankful that nothing happened to my sisters, but you can imagine what happened to me that night. Never again did I leave my sister's home alone. Plus, I was only a kid myself left at home alone with two younger sisters.

My mother got her a new boyfriend and he was coming over to dinner. We had to make sure we were on our best behavior when he got there. The doorbell rang and her new boyfriend entered the house. My mom had been cooking for a while waiting on her new friend. Now it was time to sit down at the table and we were ready to eat. As we were fixing our plates, I reached in front of me to get a biscuit and my mom said, "what do you say" and I said "excuse me biscuit" in a sarcastic tone. I got that look she thought only I could see so I explained the biscuits are in front of me, I didn't cross over anyone's plate. When the new boyfriend left, I got the beating of a lifetime. I was dancing around on that floor for a while.

Well, my mother moved again to the new projects. I didn't see much difference in old and new projects myself. In those days, children knew none of the adult's business because it wasn't our business. We moved to Denmark Street in the new projects which was the next street over from Mother Pearlie. I felt better living closer to my grandmother. I didn't like being left at home alone with my sisters. I was always afraid but had to be brave for them.

My little sister was light skinned and everyday a bunch of girls would chase her home from school. One day they all lined up on the hill behind the house. The ringleader was grabbing each girl's hand and pulling them saying "come on fight her". I had just about enough of my sister running home every day, so I stepped out the backdoor to see the mob trying to fight my baby sister.

I told the ringleader, that if you want to fight her, you can fight her, but if anybody else jumped in it, I was in the fight too. No one got up to fight her and eventually they all left the hill and went home.

Living with my grandmother, we really couldn't do much because according to our faith everything was a sin. There wasn't much to do so we joined the community center and played basketball which was my favorite sport. We had great team spirit and we enjoyed going to the center. By this time, my mother had moved to Chicago Heights. We were now living with our grandmother, Mother Pearlie and grandfather, Daddy Will. We didn't have much money while my mother was in Chicago Heights. So, to survive, I cleaned my teachers houses on Saturdays. I also pressed and curled hair to make money. I took the money I earned to buy fabric so I could make my clothes. My mom was trying to find a better life for us, and my grandparents didn't have enough money to support us with the things we needed. We barely had enough food to eat, but we never went one day without food. My grandparents had six grandchildren to feed.

My grandfather helped build the church in Faro, North Carolina and we road along with him many a day while they were building the church. One day, he came home, and he said God called him to preach and he was going to start his own church. He drove around looking for his church building, and he finally found this building covered with trees and weeds. This wouldn't have been my choice, but he cleaned it off and started his own church. I was the choir director, Sunday school teacher to the kids and in every program. My grandfather baptized us all in the name of the Father, in the name of the Son and in the name of the Holy Ghost.

My grandmother also had a prayer band that traveled from house to house. The children were supposed to be tarrying for the Holy Ghost. Of course, kids never do what they are supposed to be doing. Instead of praying for forgiveness of sin and for the Holy Ghost, I was peeping and watching what was going on in that room. One time we went with her to the prayer band and I can honestly say, I have seen some folk delivered from their sins and healed from their ailments. We witnessed a drunk coming into the prayer band one night. By the time those sisters finished laying on hands and praying over her, she was slain in the spirit and was laid out on the floor being purged. Stuff was coming out of her mouth. I can tell you when she got up off that floor, she wasn't drunk anymore and started running for Jesus, she never drank again.

We stayed with our grandparents for a while and one day we were told we had to go to Chicago to be with our mother and the three grandsons had to go to Baltimore to be with their mother. It was a sad occasion leaving my grandparents and leaving my classmates. This was the last summer we would be together.

CHAPTER 2

Reunited

Well, it's time to go to Chicago Heights, Illinois. My grandfather Willie Ward gave us a ride to Raleigh Durham Airport in Raleigh Durham, North Carolina. Della, Nita and I had to walk to the airport's runway to board the plane. This is our first airplane ride and none of us knew what was instore for us while we were on this plane called the Piedmont Airline. Riding down the runway wasn't that bad, but when the nose of that plane tipped up in the air, the plane hit every air pocket it could find. My sisters literally cried all the way to Chicago. I did everything I could to stop them from crying and I did everything I could to stop myself from crying. Sometimes, being the big sister sucks.

My mother met us at the airport and boy we were glad to see her. She had been in Chicago Heights, Illinois for a little while and had survived the 1967 snowstorm on top of that. The first thing mom did was take us to get a footlong hotdog, and boy it was a sight to see and very delicious. We would be living on Shields Avenue. My mom rented the apartment in Chicago Heights from Gerald Corbin. We lived in the front upstairs apartment and he and his family lived in the back-apartment upstairs. We eventually became the babysitter.

We arrived in Chicago Heights on July 7, 1970 and I had a few concerns about being pulled out of school in North Carolina because all my friends were left back at home. On my first day at Bloom High School all I could see were dogs in the school, patrolling the hallways. I had never in my life seen anything like this before. There was something going on because of the civil rights movement. Back in North Carolina, we couldn't watch TV because it was the first cousin to the devil. This left us out of being informed on what was happening in the world. So, I was literally clueless as to what was going on.

I had so many school credits when I came to Chicago Heights, that I had to take only two PE classes and two

English classes. I took other classes though because I was going to college to be a nurse. Well, it was time to go to prom in the spring of 1971. I didn't know anyone except the kids in my classroom, but to my surprise a guy from the school asked me to the prom. I was very skeptical about going to prom with someone I didn't know. This guy was very nice. He would buy my dress, shoes, get my flowers and everything! But I still didn't feel comfortable going to prom with him since I was new in the city and hadn't had the opportunity to get to know anyone. Therefore, to prevent from hurting his feelings, I told him I would go out with him on graduation night. I also told him we had to go out of town because I didn't want anyone to see me out with him.

My mother bought me a navy-blue hot pant outfit. I got my hair done and I was ready for my date. When Kenny pulled up in front of the house, I saw someone else in his car. It was Robert and Doris. These guys took us downtown in Chicago. We went to a restaurant that they said turned at the top, but they wouldn't let us dine in the restaurant. I guess we didn't have reservations. We finally found a restaurant where we could sit down and dine, and Robert and I did all the talking, all the eating, and all the laughing. We arrived home safely and it wasn't a bad date night.

When we lived in North Carolina, my mother worked nights and I was home alone a lot at night with my sisters. My mother was the woman that always had to have a man in her life. I had a new daddy it seemed like every weekend. Her style of men ran the gamut. They went from quartet singers to the Insurance man. I know every family needed some type of insurance, but this man was over our house a lot. How much insurance does one family need? He was light skinned and everyone called him Bitty Pudding. Well, he had a son that checked on us and eventually one day when my mother was at the store, he paid us a visit. It wasn't a wellbeing check this time and I didn't know what was going on. I was around 12 years old and can remember thinking to myself, where is my mother. He had me on my bed with my legs in the air and caused great pain down there. I can hear him saying "I'm almost done". This continued to happen for a while and then Bitty Pudding decided he was moving to Chicago. And yes, you're right, my mother went with him.

So, after we arrived that day from the airport to our new home in Chicago Heights, someone was eager to see me. Yes, he went to Chicago with his father, Bitty Pudding. The first thing he asked my mother for, was permission to take me to a party with him. In my mind, I'm saying, say no momma, say no. Well, the answer was sure she can go with you to the party. Make sure nothing happens to my child now. He replied, "I got her Deen." My mother didn't realize he really had me. This abuse started all over again. I'm not sure where his girlfriend was, but we stayed all night at his apartment, and he took me home the next morning after preparing me breakfast.

I never got pregnant when this was happening in North Carolina, but in Chicago, I got pregnant. I was afraid to let my sisters see me undress, I got sleepy the same time every day. My mother worked at Tinley Park Mental Hospital and I was so terrified that I thought the cough medicine in the medicine cabinet called

Expectorant was a clue my mother knew I was pregnant. Cortez, yes that is his name, went to the doctor on 16th street and came back with some pills and told me to take them. I wasn't prepared for what would happen to me.

I didn't know what to expect from taking those pills. I actually thought my period would just come on so I took them. After a few days while in class at Bloom High School, I got very sick and had to go to the nurse's office. I was in so much pain, I fell asleep and missed my bus home. When I awaken, I went to the bathroom and while sitting there, a big blob of something fell out of me. I was so scared and didn't know what to do. After I got home, I told Cortez what had happened, and it seemed like he really wasn't concerned about what I had just experienced. He wanted to have me again and again and again. I told him I had just been through a traumatic experience, but he didn't care. Meanwhile, I eventually ended up pregnant again.

My mother's boyfriend was going off on me because mom told him I was pregnant. He didn't know it was his own son's doing. I just stood there waiting for him to finish and I didn't say a word. It was just too much to handle at that time. I never told who the father was because I watched what my mother did to get this man and this news would have caused an upset on their relationship.

My school had a work study program, and I had an opportunity to participate in the program. My assignment from school was to report to Happy Hour Preschool in the Heights for my work study program. After I arrived at the school and opened the door to enter in, I was kissed by this strange man talking smack. I put this dude in his place and was met by a lady that asked me if my baby was a girl to name her Avies. Wow, what a greeting I received at this school on my first day. Eventually, I got to know the guy that kissed me a little better and we worked well together helping out the little kids at the Day Care.

I was pregnant and Stanley had a couple of friends and we all hung out together, so I joined the crowd and we all became best friends. We hung out together every weekend, playing cards and having fun. While working at the Day Care, on our breaks Stanley would dictate letters for me to write to his brother Robert in the military. He would sometimes mention a girl named Janice in the letters we were writing. One day I asked him, who is this Janice you keep writing to your brother about and his response was it was another Janice. So, I halfway believed him.

CHAPTER 3

In Pursuit

L iving on Shields Avenue wasn't large enough for three girls. We had to sleep in the same room on bunk beds. I slept on the top and my sisters slept on the bottom. My mother eventually found us another place to stay in an area called The Hill, 26th street. I have no idea why it was called The Hill to this day. We lived downstairs and the landlord lived upstairs. I was still pregnant, working at Happy Hour Preschool. There was another guy that worked there who was very nice as well, but he didn't hang out with our crowd. I was still hanging out in Chicago Heights with my friends on Shields Avenue drinking Hopping Gator, a malt liquor. I should not have been drinking at all being pregnant with child. One evening it was getting late and it was time for me to get home, so I caught a cab ride home that night.

While this cab driver was driving, he hit every pothole in the street and ran over the railroad tracks like a crazy man. I eventually informed him it was more than just me in the back seat and you guessed it right, I went into labor that night. My mother had just put the car in the shop, and I was ready to give birth. I had no idea what was going to happen when a woman had a baby, but when those pains came, I wanted them to hit me in the head with a hammer or baseball bat. They needed to knock me out so I wouldn't feel those labor pains. I wanted my mother and I wanted that baby out of me. They had to perform a small incision to deliver my baby and it felt like I had been riding a horse. It was so painful to walk and took a while to heal. My best friend Cherry wanted me to name her Tonya, and I was asked by this lovely lady, Mrs. Miller at Happy Hour Preschool to name the baby Avies, if I had a girl. I wanted to name her Ayanna. Therefore, I combined all the names together and named her Avies Ton Ayanna Ward and we call her Tonya. She was born a beautiful baby with swollen eyes, probably from the Hopping Gator Malt Liquor.

I was off work for a while, and I missed my coworkers. There was this young man named Gregory and they called him Honky that worked at the preschool. One day, he paid me a visit while I was out on maternity leave. Something happened when I opened the door. My hair was all over my head in a huge afro and he looked bedazzling. It was like I was seeing him for the first time. After that moment I realized that I actually missed seeing him at work and gave him a big hug. We eventually began to date. He was a Taurus and he was a very good boyfriend. He paid a lot of attention to me and always showed his loved and affection for me in public and private. He lived on Wentworth Avenue and I never told my mother that little piece of information. Our friendship was going well. We had a lot of fun together, but one day he wasn't home, and I didn't see him for over a month and I didn't know where he was.

Meanwhile, Robert returned home from the Army and the first person he wanted to see was me. I didn't find out this piece of evidence until later, but the brothers Stanley and Robert had a bet that Robert wasn't going to get next to me. Even though Honky wasn't around, I was still missing him very much. However, this Robert dude, kept coming around. He would walk the tracks from Chicago Heights to 26th street, the Hill in Chicago Heights to see me. He also started hanging out with us; me, Stanley and Pantrell. We hung out at Pantrell's house most of the time, because they always had my baby.

Poppa Barnes was a hunter and would bring home a coon and Momma Barnes would cook it. That was the ugliest thing I have ever seen in my life and no; I didn't want any. Whatever Poppa Barnes brought home Momma Barnes would cook it and dress it up real pretty, with an apple in the mouth and everything. I still didn't want any coon or any wild game meat. Momma Barnes had hot flashes all the time and kept the air conditioner running in the window. She even kept it running in the wintertime. She worked in Manteno at night and one day we gave her a ride to work. Our instructions from Momma Barnes were not to do any drag racing on our way home.

Well, Pantrell and Robert paid no attention to those strict instructions. As soon as Momma Barnes got out the car, they started racing the engines and looking at each other like rivals. These guys had rocks for brains, they didn't listen to Momma Barnes at all. Before the Manteno hospital doors closed behind Momma Barnes, there was great anticipation that one of them would burn the other up racing down the road that night. They lined up, side by side in the highway, engines were hot and ready to take off. The cars were rocking because they were racing the engine, but not taking off yet. I reminded Robert we were not supposed to do any drag racing and before I knew it, we were off to the races. Pantrell forgot there was an end to the road, and that you had to either turn right or left. He couldn't stop his car in time to make the turn. Pantrell ended up in the ditch that night with his car. Robert was also fast approaching the end of the road now and noticed Pantrell was in the ditch. Robert put his arms across my chest to keep me from bouncing into the windshield and said baby, I think we are going to make it. Now we need to call for help to get Momma Barnes' car out of the ditch. Yes, we all got in a little trouble but thank God we were all safe. My mother always told us a hard head makes a soft behind.

Time was passing by and I still didn't know where Gregory was. I had not seen him in a long time, but I was still waiting for him to show up any minute now. We hadn't had an argument or anything. As a matter of fact, we never had one argument. Gregory was a lover not a fighter when it came to me. However, Robert doesn't give up, he was very persistent and continued to pursue after me. Every time I turned around Robert was at my door in the peep hole. I didn't like this dude. He was getting on my nerves. One night he talked my mother into letting him stay all night, it was because he said a building was on fire. The next time he got my mother to let him stay all night, it was because he said they were shooting outside. I couldn't believe my mother was falling for this game. On those occasions, I didn't even know he was in our house until morning. He would be sleeping on the couch all night. Every time there was a knock at the door and I looked through the peep hole, it was Robert.

One day we were all over to Momma Barnes house and he stopped me on the stairs and ask me to go steady with him. I explained that I was in a relationship with Honky and didn't want to do anything to hurt him. Al Green was playing throughout the house, "How Can You Mend a Broken Heart" and Robert politely told me that Honky wasn't here, but he was. My heart was still on Gregory and I wasn't ready to move on into a new relationship. I wasn't attracted to Robert and we were all friends just hanging out together. Robert didn't go away and he got on my last cotton-picking nerve. One day he dropped by to call on me and I still hadn't seen Honky for a long while now and I looked through the peep hole to see it was Robert again. This time when I looked through the peep hole, he had on a black brim broke down to the side and was suited all up. For some odd reason he looked a little different to me this time and I said to myself, hmm this dude is fine today. I must have been using someone else's eyeballs that day, because I saw something that I liked. Yes, Sir Re Bob.

Honky found me and asked me to braid his hair and I did. Robert came over and saw him sitting between my legs and didn't like that. He got his cronies and sent out a threat with his actions. I didn't want anything to happen to Honky, so I told him I wasn't going to do his hair anymore. What happen to Honky you ask? Well, he was accused of participating in a gang rape and had to hide out for a while until things cooled down. His family was supposed to tell me what happened, but nobody did. Therefore, Honky and I never got back together. His cousin saw me on the street one day and asked me why I did his cousin like that, but the family never told me what happened to Honky.

CHAPTER 4

An Unwelcomed Experience

Meanwhile, Robert rented a room from Big Momma up in the Heights and was conveniently located upstairs over my friend Martha's apartment. Therefore, most of the time I was at Martha's house so I could be close to Robert. Hanging around upstairs with Robert was pleasant. He treated me well and took very good care of me. He would have his grandmother buy me outfits to wear because he loved giving me presents. Then he would pay his grandmother back from using her credit card. Hanging out at Roberts apartment caused me to end up pregnant again. At this time, my mother was making plans to move back home to North Carolina. When my mother discovered I was pregnant, she wasn't having it and wanted me to get an abortion. She said I better figure out how to get the money. So, I wrote to one of my best buddies Pantrell, who was now in the Army on a buddy buddy plan with Stanley. I told him I needed money for a special test. I couldn't bring myself to tell him what I needed the money for. It was against everything I believed in.

My mother made the arrangements for me to fly to New York. I had never flown to New York before, but someone was there waiting for me at the airport. They took me to the hospital and a shocking thing happened. This baby was moving so much I held my hands on my stomach wishing the baby would stop moving. I wanted to go back home and save my baby, but I knew my mother wouldn't have that. I was sitting there nervously waiting for them to call my name. They walked me to an area in the back where rooms were partitioned off and showed me my bed. Then the nurse came and injected me with some medicine and after a while they came and removed the baby. It was like a sweat shop. In and out and on your way back home. They gave me a card that stated I had a miscarriage. When I got back to Chicago Heights, Robert wanted to know what happened to the baby. I told him I had a miscarriage. I wasn't sure if he believed me or not, but that was my story and I was sticking to it. Robert was very angry with me and broke up with me. He stayed away for a little while and suddenly, he was wanting to get married. I was working at Jones Community Center in Chicago Heights. He wanted to go and get blood work and a marriage license. I actually didn't think he would go through with it, so I just played along with the plan, because in my mind I was moving back to Goldsboro, North Carolina.

My mother was now living in Chicago Heights alone without any support with three daughters, because her boyfriend moved back to the East Coast shortly after we arrived to Chicago Heights. Prior to him leaving, he had a visit from his wife which could have possibly persuaded him to move back home. While his wife was visiting him, my mom got angry and threw a brick at his apartment door.

She threw the brick so hard that the boil on her back burst wide opened and I had to clean her up and dress the wound. She was very hurt that night. Women should not chase after married men. Chances are they are not going to leave their wives. It's just wrong to mess with married men. I promised God at 13 years old, that I would never do that. It was very hard for my mother to manage three daughters with no support system. She hung in there as long as she could, but now it was time to go. When I told Robert, we were moving back home, he had his cousin break out my mother's car window. I guess he figured that would keep us from leaving, but it didn't. Robert told my mother he was going to North Carolina also and my mother told him at least three times he was not going. Robert being the persistent man he was, stuck to his guns and eventually my mother said he could go if he helped drive. Robert told my mother he would drive all the way.

When we arrived in North Carolina, I stayed with my Aunt Lois and I slept on the floor. The next morning my uncle said, "come on let's get ready to go". I was trying to figure out where we were going. Well, we ended up at the Goldsboro Court House. I was still confused. Robert and my uncle went into the courthouse and I stayed in the car. When I figured out what was going on, it took me a while to get out of the car. This man had brought blood test results and the marriage license. I had actually never given that stuff another thought. I sat there for a while reasoning with myself thinking about how the church makes a woman feel when she is pregnant with no husband and I also felt for a man to follow me all the way to North Carolina, he must love me, so I got out of the car. It was my wedding day. I was getting married with a pair of orange flower pants on. When we got back into the court room, he told us we needed to get a physical and come back. I was married that day, August 6, 1973 to Mr. Robert Pryor.

Later on, that day we told my mother we were married and she didn't believe us. She immediately asked to see our marriage license and we showed them to her. We stayed a few more days in North Carolina and headed back to Chicago. We stopped in Baltimore on the way back so my mother could check on her job application there at the state hospital. She would resettle where the first job opportunity became available. While in Baltimore, my childhood best friend was with my daughter's farther Tez. Everyone wanted to see me, but Robert wouldn't let me leave the bedroom and go downstairs, so they came upstairs to speak and left afterwards. This should have been our honeymoon, but this was the first sign of the abuse I was about to experience as Mrs. Pryor.

CHAPTER 5

Snake In The Grass

August 1973, we arrived back in Chicago Heights, Illinois. My mother was getting all of her things together to move back home. I definitely didn't think this thing through. I didn't realize I would be left behind because now I was married. My mother gave us her apartment and furniture, Momma took Tonya with her to give us a chance to get acclimated as a married couple. Robert had a good job and I didn't have to work. I kept the house clean and we had a few credit cards from Montgomery Wards. I had our apartment laid out.

It was time to bring Tonya home now, so I had to fly to Baltimore to get her. Robert told me I had to fly there and come right back. He wouldn't let me stay for a little while; it was a turnaround trip. Tonya had her own bedroom, but she was nervous about sleeping in the room alone. So, several times during the night I would get up to comfort her. One night, I fell asleep and heard all this noise in our apartment. When I got up to see what in the world was going on that time of the night, I discovered Mr. Pryor and the boys were shooting dice in my living room. I didn't say one john brown word. I proceeded to the kitchen and put a pot of water on the stove and boiled the water. He came into the room and asked me why I was boiling water. I told him, I was raising a family in this house and he was having guys in our home, gambling. Immediately, Robert told the guys they had to leave. We were living at 1200 Wentworth Apartment 1 in Chicago Heights, IL.

We lived in Wentworth Gardens and everyone just about in the 70's was getting high on weed or something. I was too cheap to spend my money on a dime bag or nickel bag of weed. I would rather buy a bottle of Bacardi Rum, which would last me much longer than a nickel bag. That's what I did. One night, Robert wanted me to indulge and threatened to burn me if I didn't. I took one pull and when he struck a match, his match looked like the whole house was on fire. I was on the floor on my hands and knees and wouldn't get up. Robert got frantic and was calling my name. All I can remember saying was "no, no, no!" That was my first time and last time for that. He used to try and sell weed, and I would steal it and give it away to his sister. I didn't want it in the house.

We had nice neighbors living in Wentworth Gardens. I had this nice lady giving me all kinds of advice about what I should put in my hair and I should do this and I should do that. Meanwhile, my mother in-law had gotten me a job as the church secretary to Pastor John H. Rice, Sr at a church named St Bethel Missionary Baptist Church. I was pregnant and walked to work every day with Tonya by my side. One day on my way to work I forgot something and needed to go back home. To my surprise, this lady was sitting on my coach with her legs crossed and her arms strolled across the back of my couch. I thought it was strange for her to be in my house when I wasn't at home. Of course, she left immediately when I arrived. I sort of excused that incident and gave my husband the benefit of the doubt on that round.

Robert was a very jealous man. One day, we all ordered food at the church and they asked me to go and pick it up for lunch. So, Reverend Dupee let me use his car to pick up the food. Well, Robert saw me driving the car and ran me off the road with our car. I was scared my husband would damage Rev. Dupee's car and/or kill me in it. What was wrong with this man. I was only going to pick up lunch for everybody for goodness sake. There had been many instances where the children and I were out walking and Robert's friends would be driving our car around town or Robert would drive past us himself. In contrast me and the children walked to our destination.

One night we were having a party at the crib celebrating Robert's birthday. Everybody was there and everyone was having a good time. I started looking around and didn't see Robert and found him in the bedroom with a few friends and the nice neighbor lady. Robert was leaning back on the bed and the bulge in his pants was evidence of where his mind was, and it wasn't on the party. He left the party with the nice lady and a friend.

Delores, Robert's sister, was very upset with him and told him if he didn't want me, he should let me move back home with my mother in Baltimore. I was pregnant now and Robert asked me if he was the father. Afterall, he wouldn't let me stay in Baltimore long enough to even visit my mother. I told him you will find out when the baby comes. He didn't know that another nice neighbor told me what went on when I was in Baltimore getting my daughter. It might be too sexually explicit to mention for this audience. After getting this news I packed up my luggage to move back home with my mother and Robert told me I was his wife and he didn't want me to leave. He wanted another chance.

So, I continued to go to work and one morning I forgot something and had to go back home again. Robert had left before me to go to work that morning so in my mind he was at work. Well, I was wrong. When I went back home, the top latch was on the door, which could only be put on from the inside of the apartment. I was standing there with Tonya thinking what in the world is going on here.

Suddenly, this little boy runs through the hallway telling me he just saw Judy jumping out of my window. She lived in the next apartment in the building and I lived in apartment #1. Judy's boyfriend caught wind of the news and beat the living daylights out of her. He turned to give me the iron and instructed me to finish the job. I looked at her and told him, she wouldn't feel any of my licks at all because he had beat her so badly.

Here I stand, pregnant, only making $40 a week, but I knew at that moment, that I needed to get me a new apartment. I no longer wanted to live with this man. We lived in the apartment buildings called Wentworth Gardens and I knew the lady that managed Wentworth Gardens apartments. After explaining my dilemma, Mrs. Delphine gave me another apartment on the 3rd floor in the building where the office was located. Well, you guessed right. Robert moved with me. There was no getting away from this dude. We stayed there for a while and eventually had to move again. We moved into Mr.

Noble's building, across the street from the Gardens. There was water in the bathtub that wouldn't go down. Therefore, we couldn't take a bath. I had to hold Tonya all night long in my arms because we had mice running up and down the curtains all night. Tonya cried a lot especially when I left her with Robert. She started rocking and bumping her back while sitting on the couch continuously. When Mr. Noble wouldn't fix the plumbing, we had to get out of there. Robert found a place on Arnold. When I went to look at the place, I cried all day long. I didn't want to move in that shot gun house.

CHAPTER 6

Garage Apartment

Robert must have talked to his grandfather, Big Daddy about our situation, and we moved behind them at 301 East 16th street. I was about ready to deliver at this point. I was home alone a lot. Robert wouldn't let me go anywhere, so I was stuck in the house all the time. I have no idea where Robert got a waterbed from, but I had difficulty getting up off the bed. I went somewhere, probably with his mother and when I came home, I found an earring on the floor next to my waterbed and it wasn't mine. When Robert came home, I asked him to take the waterbed down or I was going to cut the bed up into shreds. He took it down that night. This marriage was very stressful.

Robert was constantly having sex outside of the marriage. He came home one day upset, after meeting his girlfriend from Chicago at his brother's house. I wasn't sure what was going on with him that day. All of a sudden, he beat me in the head with his fist and after he finished beating me, he had the nerve to ask me if he hurt the baby. He would hit me, and I would fall down and bounce back up. I bounced back up after every lick. I had seen nothing like this before in my life. In my family men didn't hit women and I had never heard them argue either. I knew I would not be able to last through all these beating from my husband. So, I started saving money and hiding it at Granny's house under her chair in the living room. I was still working as the church secretary at St Bethel.

I had no clothes to wear because I was getting big. My mother-in- law purchased me a few things to wear. Since I knew how to sew, I made my own clothes. I sewed for my sister-in-law, Delores as well. It was about time for me to deliver. My mother and my sister Stephanie came to Chicago to be with me when I had the baby. My mother brought me some fresh fish and some good ole iced tea. For some reason, I scrapped all the ice out of the freezer,

I ate all the ice out of the ice trays, and I cleaned up frantically. I eventually went to sleep and slept all night long. I was awakened early the next morning with a slight pain, so I just said ouch and went back to sleep.

This pain continued and I eventually got up and went to the bathroom. There was blood in the toilet. I called my mother and she said you are not going to work today because you just had a bloody show. I didn't know what she was talking about and I didn't go to work either. My mother took all my laundry and washed for me. When she returned, she fried me the fresh fish she brought me from Baltimore and made me a nice pitcher of iced tea. I stayed home all day refusing to go to the hospital. I remembered what they did the last time and I remembered that big clock on the wall reminding me of the next pain that was on the way. After a while, I began to lift my legs up and put them on the coffee table. My mother said, "Oh no, it's time for you to go to the hospital." On the way to the hospital, Robert ran every red light and I prayed to God we would make it to the hospital safely. Upon arrival at St. James Hospital, they put me in a room with a huge clock on the wall again. My pains were very painful now and almost unbearable. Robert was down the hall with the fathers having cheese and wine while I was experiencing the worst pain ever. This was October 1974 and my doctor went home to watch the world series. He thought it would be a minute before I delivered, not realizing I had been in labor at home all day. I had two pains I thought was going to take me out. I felt like I had to go to the bathroom and did go. While sitting there, I thought I better get up off this toilet before that pain comes again. I got back into the bed and asked God, if you help me make it through this next pain, I will be all right. With that big clock in front of me on the wall, I knew exactly when to expect the next pain and it was coming fast. I grabbed the hospital bed's headboard and said to God please help me make it through this pain. I was in the room by myself and when it came, I pushed. At that very moment, Robert came back into the room and our baby boy was coming out. Robert turned pale and almost fainted. We had a baby boy and we named him Robert Charles Pryor Jr. affectionately called June Bug.

I stayed in the hospital a few days and could finally go home. Robert picked me up and when we arrived home, he wanted to stop by Big Daddy and Granny's place first. I told him I wasn't feeling good and wanted to go home. Home was literally behind them in their backyard. The next thing I knew, Robert had stolen the baby and took him out of the house with no bottle nor diapers or anything. I called the police because this was a brand-new baby and I wasn't too keen about my baby being around people yet. The police came and saw the baby was returned and back in his crib. Robert told the police, "See he's back in his bed, Officer". The Officer politely reminded me it was his baby as well. After the police left, Robert started an argument with my mother and sister who were still there to assist me with the new baby. My Mother was explaining to Robert that I was in a lot of pain due to severe after birth pains and needed to be home in the bed. She also mentioned that taking the baby out so early may not be good for the baby. The older generation wouldn't let you go outside for 30 days after having a baby, but this was Robert's first baby and he wasn't listening to anything anyone was saying that night. Therefore, an argument escalated to the point that Robert told my mother to step outside. He was going to settle the issue. He had his gun and I am so thankful my mother didn't go out that door. My sister was very angry now and had a few choice words for him calling him redneck, fat neck, and whatever came out of her mouth that night. My mother gathered her and Tonya's things because she was taking her back to Baltimore with her. This would give us a chance to get our lives back together.

CHAPTER 7

Eye For An Eye

Robert was unemployed and we were receiving assistance from the state. The state sent us a check every month because we had almost no income coming in the household. When Robert would receive the check, he did what he wanted with it and didn't support the family with food and other household things we needed. Tonya and I lived off $40/week; the salary I made working at the church as the church secretary. One day I called ADC and told them I wanted them to put the check in my name because my children and I were not benefiting from the money. The state told me Robert was the man of the house and they couldn't put the check in my name, but I could cancel it. I told her to cancel the check because me and the kids never saw a drop of that money. When that check didn't come in the mail, he came running down to the church where I worked and asked me where was the check? I told him I didn't have the check. He argued and argued with me in the church office. He got so mad at me, that he swung his arm across my face and the corner of his watch cut my eye. I couldn't see out that eye for a while. I had to wear a patch over it until it healed. I can remember driving down one-way streets with that patch praying, "Lord please don't let me hit any cars on this one-way street."

He was so mean. He would push the stroller into the back of my heel while walking down the street, constantly running into the back of my legs. As I mentioned, I was home alone most of the time and the apartment had paneling on the wall and square tiles on the ceiling. I would sit there and count the paneling and tiles in the ceiling to pass the time. Being continuously abused, I continued saving my money at Granny's house. Every time I was able to get out of the house, I would take a piece of clothing or something I needed to take with me when I escaped this horrible situation. I had purchased a trunk and left it over to my best friend, Martha's house, and I began packing clothes in it every chance I could.

One day, my mother-in-law was going to Chicago and asked me if I wanted to go with them. I said "no". This was my chance, and I thank God they didn't take June Bug with them. I had already asked for my money and I hurried along and got out of that house with my baby and my sewing machine. While escaping, I didn't tell my mother my plans because I didn't want my mother to lie for me. She didn't know if I was dead or alive for a week. Martha and Henry Rice Jr. hid me in Chicago for a week and put me on the plane the following week bound for Baltimore.

When I arrived in Baltimore, I slept in my mother's unfinished basement. I didn't want to occupy her upstairs living space. I kept the upstairs clean and slept in her unfinished basement, me, June Bug, and the dog. I went to the Salvation Army and found two twin beds. I purchased some linoleum and installed it in a little section for me and my baby. Tonya slept upstairs with her aunties. I immediately looked for a job and an

Janice F. Pryor

apartment. I also exercised to get rid of the baby fat I had gained. I made sure I cleaned my mother's house, cooked, paid the bills, and took her hot lunches periodically to work. My mother always worked the second shift. She never cared for the day shift.

I had been in Baltimore for a while now and the family in Chicago Heights wanted me to come there for Christmas. It was so cold in Chicago Heights that winter, when you went outside your nose froze. After the holiday, I told them I was ready to go back to Baltimore. I'm sure they were hoping I would stay, but it was just too much for me to handle the abuse. I was abused physically, mentally, and spiritually. They put me on the plane and back to Baltimore, Maryland I went. While living with my mother, my sisters weren't doing what they were supposed to do, and I was actually getting tired of cleaning up behind them all the time. One day, I got a call from one of my classmates and she told me if I wanted my husband I better come home. I thought about the situation I was in and felt I would go back and see if it would be better this time.

Robert and Delores drove to Baltimore to pick us up in Big Daddy's Riviera with dual mufflers. We rented a U-Haul and Robert drove me to Brooklyn, New York so I could see my father before we returned back to Chicago Heights. Delores was driving and when she approached the bridge with all the lights shining bright at night, she began screaming with great fear of driving across the bridge. Robert told her she better not stop driving on that bridge and that she better keep driving until she got across it. My father lived in Brooklyn and we were quickly approaching his place. When we arrived, my father told me the doctor asked him to stop drinking. His interpretation was to stop drinking brown liquor and start drinking clear liquor. It was truly a blessing that Robert took me to Brooklyn because that was the last time I saw my father alive. He literally drank himself to death. When we left New York, Deloris was sick, and Robert was tired. So, I had to take the first drive. I loved driving and I practically drove all the way home. I had to get off of 80 and drop down to the Ohio Turnpike. When Robert woke up, he reminded me I wasn't supposed to get back on the Turnpike.

However, I had to in order to get back to Illinois. The next state was Indiana and as soon as we got in Indiana, we had trouble with the car. I had to pull over on the side of the road and Robert looked under the car's hood to see if he could figure out what was going on with the car. Robert was a lightweight mechanic. He could do anything he set his mind to though. We were near the next exit, so we got off and went to the Hotel. Meanwhile, Robert called Big Daddy and explained our dilemma. We stayed all night in Indiana, and I was out like a light. I had driven all the way from New York and this sister was tired. When I woke up, we were ready to hit the road again. Robert took the wheel and brought us home from Indiana.

CHAPTER 8

Loss Of A Father

It was good being back home in the city of Chicago Heights. We were getting ready to make that grand entrance by driving down Wentworth Avenue. You would have thought that the corner of Wentworth and 14th street was a famous street in Hollywood, California. The street was lined with people on both sides as we road down Wentworth, and Robert raising his Black Power fist to the people all the way down the street, More Power to The People. My husband had to ride down Wentworth to let everyone know he was rolling back in town. This was very frustrating because I never understood why every time we got back in town we had to drive down Wentworth Avenue. We finally arrived at home after the parade and I came back to the same little garage apartment behind Big Daddy and Granny, but it was mine. Now that I was settled in, I needed to figure out how to get me some income to help my husband because we had bills and two babies. After a while, I was told I could get some general assistance, so I went to the office to apply for assistance. When I arrived at the General Assistance office, they gave me an application. I filled out all the paperwork and got interviewed directly afterwards by one of the staff in the office. After we finished the interview, they sent me to a job the same day. The name of the company was Tech OPS Landauer. Landauer hired me the same day. That's the way God works, and I thanked God for favor.

After working at Landauer for a little while, I received a call that my father was dead. So, back to New York we went for his funeral. Robert asked Uncle Melvin to go along so he wouldn't have to drive the whole way alone. Melvin took the wheel after Robert got him on the Turnpike and he was driving with no license. I guess a lot of people did that back in the day. He was also driving about 90 miles an hour. My momma would say, "driving like a bat out of hell". Robert raised his head and looked at how fast Melvin was driving and told him he had to slow down. He had no money for tickets, and we wanted to arrive to New York in one piece. Uncle Melvin didn't know how to read either, but he was always willing to help. I guess he knew how to follow the main traffic flow on the turnpike, or we would have ended up in Timbuktu.

After we arrived in New York, the fellows wanted to hang out. So, me and the kids stayed at the crib with my Aunties and Uncles. The next day was the funeral and I wanted to make sure everything was ready. When we arrived at the funeral home and I walked in that room where my fathered laid. I remember my first thought was, that doesn't look like my father. His skin was a dark complexion and he didn't resemble himself at all. When the services began, I thought back over my life and remembering how badly I wanted to spend some time with my father. But I never got the opportunity unless he was visiting my grandmother, Ma Mary, his mother. I wrote him letters and he never received them. I longed to have a relationship with my father, but he died before I could get the opportunity. Yes, they had to take me out of the funeral home because I was cutting up bad and they put me in the car. My daddy was gone and everyone else was able to spend time with him except me. I never got to develop a healthy relationship with him. My father was buried in a military cemetery in Brooklyn, New York. Driving to the burial was a very dangerous ride. They were driving 100 miles an hour, or it seemed like they were. Robert Pryor wasn't going to get separated from the funeral car. He passed people up, he was weaving in and out of traffic, throwing on breaks, riding their bumper, whatever else it took to keep up with the funeral directors. Afterwards, we went back to my stepmother's house and she was looking for a token to give me to remember him by. She looked around the room. She said I don't have anything to give you, so she gave me some rings. I said thank you, but I wasn't looking for anything. What I wanted was dead and gone; my daddy.

We had to get back home because we had to return to work. I was working in the receiving department at

Landauer. My responsibility was to open the mail, sort the mail, and package the radiation monitoring badges into bundles of 16. When we came to a certain number it was called a process and taken into the darkroom so they could cut the badges open and load the film in a developing tray. After the film was developed, it was spliced together and put on a reel to be read on a machine that measured the film's density, so the dose of radiation could be calculated. I was making $2.30/hour. I worked hard and learned fast. They would come and stand around to watch me work. I remembered the account numbers by heart and was dedicated to my responsibilities. After working a year, it was time for my raise. I was excited to see how much I would get. When my supervisor called me to the side, he told me I was getting a 10-cent raise, I almost fell to the floor. I couldn't believe I had worked so hard and all I was getting was a 10-cent raise.

Anyway, they liked how I worked, and they wanted to know what church I went to because they needed to hire more blacks. It was only two blacks there when I was hired. I told them I belonged to St. Bethel Missionary Baptist Church. I gave them my Pastor's name. This was the beginning of a relationship between Landauer and Pastor Rice. Pastor Rice referred several Blacks to be hired at Landauer.

Getting to work sometimes was a challenge. We had a Chevy Chevelle and it never started for me in the wintertime. I would be outside for 15 minutes trying to start that car and Robert would walk outside and start it right away and off to work I went. Working at Landauer was a new experience for me. It was my first job. They would ask questions like, "So, are you going to have another baby next year?" I would reply nicely, "I am married, and my husband and I will decide if we are going to have another child next year." Another question was, "Why are your teeth so white?" Under my breath I would say, "Maybe because I brush my teeth, I don't know." I worked a lot of hours and sometimes I would bring my kids to work on Saturdays and make them a pallet on the floor because I didn't have a babysitter.

CHAPTER 9

The Unexpected

Well, we were still living in Chicago Heights at 301 E. 16th Street. June Bug was attending Governor State University Day Care where his Auntie Delores worked. Delores was good help for me. She was always there for me with the kids. One day, she brought June Bug home and said he had peed outside while playing on the college campus. I wonder where he got that from? However, June Bug was mad because she was telling on him and he picked up a brick and threw it at me. The others didn't even come in the house. They turned around and left, and June Bug and I had a good ole deliverance service. We never had that problem again. June Bug was very busy, especially at night when he should've been sleeping. He would empty out my purse and one night he got my cigarettes and tried to light them on the stove. He had his first shouting lesson that night. That scared me for real. This apartment was like the size of a garage and they turned it into an apartment. We lived downstairs, and it was right next to the alley.

One night, we were all sleeping, and we heard something like a loud bang. We all jumped up and there was a huge alley rat knocked out in front of the stove. He was a big one and it was time to move. Living there we were trying to kill roaches downstairs. Robert's uncle, who lived upstairs, always said he didn't have any. It was a losing battle. Robert finally convinced Uncle Jura he had roaches also, by spraying under his sink. Roaches were everywhere. Uncle Jura was like, "good Lord where did they come from?" We eventually were able to get rid of the infestation.

Robert was a bootleg mechanic and had an old car he wanted to get rid of. He sold the car as is, to a friend. Well, after a couple of days his friend didn't want the car anymore and tried to give it back. They argued out front and yep, I was looking out the window with my pistol. If anything had gone down somebody would have been shot and hopefully it wasn't my husband. 301 E. 16th Street wasn't the best of memories, but God was still good.

One day, I was hanging out at Granny's house and Big Daddy received a phone call. He and Robert were outside working on our car. I immediately ran outside to tell Big Daddy the phone was for him and at that very moment the heater hose flew off the car I was scolded over a fourth of my body. My goodness they heard me scream from 301 E 16th street to downtown Chicago Heights. My son would have been scalded with all that antifreeze if I had not stepped back when I did. God knew I could take it better than my child. That's how I feel about that situation. That would have damaged my son for life. They took me into Granny's house and rubbed butter all over me, I felt like a fried chicken. Then they wanted to put salt all over me. Our car was down, and nobody took me to the hospital. I didn't sleep well that night, I was in so much pain. I tossed and turned all night long making sure I didn't sleep on that side. I guess I eventually went to sleep.

The next morning, I had big blisters all over my body hanging everywhere full of fluid. When Robert woke up and saw my condition, he found a way to get me to Dr. Watkin's office. The pain was unbearable, I paced the floor constantly trying not to cry. The doctor saw my condition and called me ahead of the other patients that day. Lord knows I was thankful. He burst all the blisters and put some yellow stuff all over me. I guess maybe Sulphur, can't say for sure. I couldn't wear any clothes, so I wore dusters. They were loosely fit and didn't irritate my wounds. Robert didn't like me wearing those dusters, but I had nothing else I could fit in. After those burns healed, my pigmentation wasn't the same and I was embarrassed for anyone to see my arm's condition.

After a while, I had bad headaches and would get dizzy occasionally. Momma Nita encouraged me to go to the doctor. I made my appointment and on the first visit the doctor looked at me and actually slapped me. I asked him "Why did you slap me?" He said you have been picking at this sore. I told him it would never heal. When I put medicine on it, the scab would get soft and stick in my hair, so I had to pick the scab off. The doctor recommended that I have surgery, and we scheduled it. After a few weeks I was in surgery.

They were doing the surgery with local anesthesia and I could hear everything they were saying during surgery. My head was covered up and I could actually feel them cutting and pulling the skin away, with no pain of course.

I could tell by the movement of my head. I guess they had cut so much out that the stitch broke and they had to get a thicker thread to close the wound. To cover the stiches, you would think they would have given me a gauze that wouldn't stick to the stitches. It should have been anything except cloth gauze, but they didn't. Therefore, when I cleaned my wound it pulled at the stitches and I ended up with a scare in my temple the size of a nickel. I cried because no hair would grow there. I had to go back to work soon so I had to buy me a wig to hide my scar. One morning on the way to work Robert said you need to do something with that thang on your head. Tears formed in my eyes because that was the best I could do. I couldn't do my hair yet because the wound was still open, and I still had bandages on my wounds but needed to get back to work as soon as possible.

I did mention it was time for us to move, and we moved to 490 East 17th Street in Chicago Heights. I was still working at Landauer, and Robert was working at Chemical Glass.

Robert liked to throw parties and we had one in the basement one night. The music was nice, and Robert was DJing. When the party was over, I went downstairs and Robert was just sitting there staring into space. I shook him and said, "Hey dude, the party is over you need to come upstairs." He eventually came upstairs and went to bed. He was drinking heavy. There was always someone over hanging out. It was also a lot of pill popping going on. I always kept my figure a 36-23-36. I measured myself daily to make sure I had the measurement I desired. Some of us were going to the fat doctor who looked like he, himself weighed about 500 lbs. We also were taking diet pills like Black Beauties or Christmas Trees to lose weight. I am so thankful the Lord kept his hands on me during my low self-esteem years. I was already skinny.

Why in the world did I think I was fat? My In-laws always called me fat, but actually I wasn't. I had big legs and that was it. To this day, I do not like taking pills and I am still grateful to my Lord and Savior for keeping me. We must learn to love ourselves exactly the way God created us. We get caught up in what we think some men are looking for. Sometimes we, single women think that we can change the man. Let us concentrate on enhancing our inner beauty, building our spiritual life while we wait on the Lord. Allow them to see Jesus through you. Jesus never makes a mistake.

One night, my husband came home, and I was in the bed already. After a while I felt wet and thought, this man has peed in the bed. I immediately got up and turned on the light. To my surprise there was blood everywhere. My husband's arm was sliced open. I called his parents and asked them to please come over and help me get him to the hospital. They came over, but I had closed the wound and bandaged him up already. I desperately wanted to get him to the hospital. They sat with me for a while and went home. The next morning, I checked him, and he was still out like a light and appeared all right, so I went to work. When Robert woke up out of his drunken state, he called me at work and asked me what happen. It wasn't much I could tell him because I wasn't with him and I had not a clue what happened to his arm. After visiting the emergency room that day, they told him he had to wait to have surgery because the wound was open too long. They were afraid an infection would set up if they did surgery.

He eventually had surgery to correct his arm, but it didn't stop his partying. This accident to his arm could have been really bad had a main artery been cut. There is something about the grace of God. Robert's drinking problem caused him to wreck our gray Buick LaSabre and he was becoming very violent. One day, he was so angry with me he put his hands around my neck and choked me. I could feel myself going out, not sure how I would get out of this one. I knew he would kill me this time and as I was beginning to black out, everything was turning white, I turned my head to the right and June Bug was standing in the doorway with a butcher knife that was bigger than him. Robert looked up and saw his son standing there holding that knife because his dad was choking his mother to death and dropped me to the floor. I can't imagine what was going through our son's mind. Do I kill my daddy and save my mother? That was a very sad day for me. I told him he needed to stop drinking the Bull (Schlitz Malt Liquor) because the bull was causing him to get into too much stuff that was affecting our family.

With everything going on, I told Robert I wanted a divorce because things weren't getting better, they were getting worse. I took my rings off and gave them to him and told him we needed to end this marriage. He asked me to give him another chance. However, what came out of his mouth didn't mean a thing to me this time. I had heard it all before. Meanwhile, Robert had purchased another get around car, but he wouldn't let me drive it. I was still working at Landauer and needed to get back and forth to work. Gloria worked there as well, and I asked her if I could ride to work with her. This lasted for a little while but eventually Gloria told me she couldn't give me a ride anymore because she was always late. Gloria being late didn't matter to me. I just needed a ride to work. I came home crying wondering how in the world was I going to get to work now. It was a Friday night, and I told God if he would bless me with a car to get back and forth to work and church I would get rid of my cigarettes. When Robert came home that evening, I gave him my cigarettes and asked him to take me to the bank and he did. When I arrived, they gave me an application to apply for credit.

After I filled out the application, the Bank Manager told me to go and find me a car and come back to the bank. I took Big Daddy with me, and Big Daddy checked out everything on the car, including the smoke's color coming out of the exhaust pipe. I went back to the bank and I purchased a yellow Buick. This was my first car and I never smoked again. God provided for me and I kept my promise. Many of us pray and ask God to bless us with this and that and after we receive our blessing, we break our promise to God. I would not break my promise to God. I try very hard to be a woman of my word and I try hard not to promise something that I cannot keep. I was rolling now and was happy because this was my car. Praise the Lord.

CHAPTER 10

The Addiction

R obert came home and talked to me regarding what was going on in his life. He sat me down and explained his job had put him in a special program called the Alcoholic Anonymous Association (AAA) and the steps that had to be completed. Therefore, he needed to tell me what was happening in his life. He explained that The Bull was not causing all this trouble in our family, it was cocaine. I didn't know what to say except, I was ready to go. He explained that me and the kids needed to go through a program at Ingalls Memorial Hospital. So, we went to all the programs and completed the requirements for AAA. We also attended individual and family counseling. Because Robert had so much bottled up in him, I told him he couldn't discipline the children anymore, because he was too angry and too strong. While going through this, Robert had the nerve to tell me he wanted more children and he went as far as to tell me, I was depriving him of children. I had two children already, Robert Jr. and Avies. In my mind, with these problems, I couldn't see bringing another baby into this house. However, Mr. Pryor got to work and threw away all my birth control medicine; the pills, cream and the suppositories. He left all the containers in the same place, so I wouldn't know what he had done until I went to take my pill. I had to contact the doctor and got refills right away. I wasn't trying to have any more kids.

After a while, a strange thing began to happen. I would stay on my monthly for weeks at a time. I was also having a lot of abdomen pain. With these symptoms, I knew I needed to go to the doctor and get this checked out. It was happening too frequently. After my visit to the doctor, he told me I had Fibroid Tumors and he wanted to take me off the pill to see if they were growing. I had no problem with this request because my thought process was since I've been on the pill for years, I was covered and wouldn't get pregnant right away. So, I had no worries, right? I was covered and therefore was assured every night I was still protected by nine years of taking the pill. Wrong answer. Mr. Pryor got busy and was laying out sexy pajamas and setting the mood. Although, his favorite was the long black gown with the split up the middle. He became so loving, I forgot what I was doing. He laid it on thick. Playing all the right music, singing with that funny voice of his. Too funny, I was trapped and couldn't get out. I had no defense, he was giving me something I longed for, some good ole fashion loving. I forgot all about the pills, cream, and suppositories.

One morning, Robert woke up all bright eyed and bushy tailed coming into the living room like a news announcer. He said, Jan you are pregnant! I immediately said, "No I'm not." He said yes you are Jan, you are pregnant. Well, I needed to prove this joker was wrong because I wasn't pregnant. When I went back to the doctor to see if my fibroid tumors were growing, the doctor told me I was pregnant. I could have fell off that table with this news and I cried and told the doctor, this is your baby. I said that because he was the one that took me off the pill. I didn't realize how this may have sounded to others on the other side of the door and the doctor replied, do not say that too loudly others may hear you. I literally cried for 3 months. I didn't want to lose my job and had several concerns.

I told my job I was pregnant and discovered there was no insurance for pregnant women or out on maternity leave. I started talking loudly and expressing my concerns on the job, not having insurance wasn't fair. We could be driving to work, and something happen to us and we have no coverage. Eventually, Landauer took care of providing benefits for pregnant women. My pregnancy was very difficult, I still had the fibroids and I got sharp pains late at night called red flashes and that wasn't enough, I also had an infection on my right foot where it itched every night. I couldn't wear a shoe on that foot, but I kept working, wearing house shoes every day to work. I was really pregnant now and wanted to make sure when the baby came, I would have a washer and dryer, so I saved money towards this goal.

Mr. Pryor was still doing his thing and I wasn't happy about what was happening in the house. Robert Jr. (June Bug) was acting out and wasn't coming straight home from school, causing Tonya to get spanked. He played a lot of little pranks on his sister. She was responsible to make sure they were in the house after school and her brother was not cooperating. June Bug would poke holes in the kitchen chair and say his sister did it. He would take pictures with the camera and say his sister did it. He was also very hyper and was always running through the house thinking he was the karate kid. After coming home one day, I discovered Robert had disciplined the children again. I told him if it happened again, I would beat him. I had to eventually take June Bug off of sugar and peanut butter. This little dude was off the chain. I was often going to bed alone. My husband worked swing shift or was gone somewhere with his friends. However, at night when he would finally come home from his night out, he would wake me up in the middle of the night by putting pickled pig feet next to my head. I would wake up half asleep and eat those pickled pig feet in the middle of the night. During this pregnancy, I also wanted chitterlings every weekend. I would put my big belly on that sink and clean chitterlings every weekend. I had really weird cravings while carrying this baby.

I was still saving a little money to purchase a washer and dryer. So, when the baby came, I would have appliances to keep the baby clothes cleaned and our clothes. I was still going to church praising my God even though I was going through so much and it seemed like I had no way out, no help, and no shoulder to cry on. I pressed my way and I kept remembering that my grandmother told me that God didn't honor divorce. I kept thinking, why would God want anyone to stay in a marriage where there is so much discord? I knew there was an answer some-where to show me what to do. I needed to figure out the answers to my problems. I needed to get me and these kids out of this very bad situation. We had supported Mr. Pryor in all the programs and never missed a night of counseling. I began to read my bible. I read and read, trying to find some answers for myself. One night, I was reading, and I ran across a scripture where it stated that God's will is that you have peace. I also read God will forgive you for everything except blasphemy against the Holy Spirit. This was truly a revelation. I was still in the State of Illinois with no blood family, because as stated, I am just a country girl from Goldsboro, North Carolina trying to survive. Growing up in Goldsboro, North Carolina, we learned to love God; honor your parents so you can live long upon this land and that a good name is rather to be chosen than fine silver and gold.

When my mother moved to Chicago to be with her best friend for a while, we were left behind to live with our grandparents while she was away. My mother was in Chicago and my cousins' mother was in Baltimore with her best friend. We were left with our grandparents during this period. While in my grandparent's house, I had never seen my uncles or my grandfather yell or beat my aunts or my grandmother. They always worked together for bettering the family. So, this abuse I was experiencing with my husband was new. At first, because I suffered with low self-esteem, I thought it was something I was doing to cause my husband to beat me, cheat on me, disrespect me, and tear me down mentally, physically and spiritually. Therefore, I began to try and figure out what I could possibly be doing to bring all this grief on myself. I thought I was a good wife. I did everything he told me to do. He said jump I jumped because I wanted to be submissive, the way my grandmother was. I watched her take care of her husband and I wanted to take care of my husband, just like her. I didn't want my husband to ever say I wasn't a good wife. I didn't want him to go lacking for anything. I put him first, because he was the head. Regardless of all the efforts of trying to be the best wife ever, our problems continued.

One day, the baby was really acting up. I didn't feel well and stayed home from work. My brother-in-law called to check on me and he asked me how I was doing. I told him I was waiting for him to come home. Not realizing it was my brother-in-law and not my husband.

Stanley said, "Uh oh, I better call Robert and tell him he need to get home right away." Sure enough, I was feeling bad and felt I was in the early stages of labor.

Therefore, I checked my bank account to see if I had saved enough money for the washer and dryer. I pulled up my bank account, even though I was in pain. They were becoming more frequent now and I looked at my account balance and it was a big fat egg. Yes, you are right again, it was a zero balance. My husband had gone and spent all the money I was saving for the washer and dryer. I think that pushed me right over the edge and those labor pains became unbearable. I was in so much pain I didn't feel like arguing about the money. I learned a valuable lesson that day. I knew I had to separate the money between the two of us, or me and the kids were not going to survive.

Off to the hospital we went. Saint James Hospital located in Chicago Heights. They admitted me and took me straight to the room. This baby was two weeks late. She was supposed to be delivered in December 1980 around Christmas time. I guess she took her own sweet time coming here. Robert named her Monique Faye Pryor. When she was born she went straight to sleep. Because of the infection on my right foot, they kept my baby away from me three days in isolation. My family doctor, Dr. Watkins, came in and told those nurses to give me my baby. I had carried her nine months and there was no need to isolate me from my baby now. Doctor Watkins gave me two shots. One was for my right foot which seemed like it healed overnight and the second one was for my rare blood type which felt like it was to the bone. They brought Monique to my room, and she was the butter ball I expected. In those days, the hospital kept you at least five days and it was time to go home now. My doctors had planned to complete the surgery regarding those tumors 30 days after delivery. My sister-in-law Delores would help me with the children when I went back for surgery. Well, while I was in the hospital after surgery, June Bug and Tonya got the measles. Robert and his sister had to hold down the fort while I was in the hospital and they were real troupers handling this dilemma.

CHAPTER 11

Our First Home

While living on 17th Street, I would periodically bring work home to make extra money. We manufactured radiation monitoring badges and processed them for reading and calculating the dose of exposure. One night, I went to sleep and had a dream that my sister was choking on Thermoluminescent Dosimeter (TLD) chip, which was one of the badges we made on the job. I was not sure what that dream was about at the time. I did not understand it until I received a called from my mother. She had to rush to Texas because my sister had accidentally taken an overdose of medication. I am so thankful it was caught in time and her life was saved. She was in Texas on one of those magazine adventures where they take these young kids from city to city to solicit orders for magazines.

One evening, we were all at home and we received a visit from our landlord. He informed us he was selling the property and wanted to give us the first opportunity to purchase the property. We lived downstairs and Robert's best friend, Henry lived upstairs. We were utterly surprised with this news and had never given a second thought regarding purchasing property. Since Henry's wife and I had a little altercation, Robert knew that wouldn't work if they became our landlords, so Robert decided we would look for property and we would use his VA benefits to purchase our property. I guess you are wondering what altercation, well, let me tell you.

One evening, I was sitting at my kitchen table reading the word of God and my children were downstairs in the basement playing. Suddenly, I hear all this noise and my upstairs neighbor was cursing out my children telling them she had cleaned up the basement. We were nasty and dirty, and the basement better be clean when they come up out of the basement. So, I'm thinking, I don't curse my children and no one else is. I closed the bible and opened the door to address the situation. She began to say the same things to me talking about we were nasty and didn't keep the basement clean. We were somewhere by the backdoor stairs and I had enough of her talk. I'm not one that will talk and talk and talk, so I did the next best thing. I pulled her tail down and we fought. Our husbands, who were best friends mind you, had to pull us apart. So, we couldn't stay there anymore.

We searched the area and found property at 251 Fredrick Drive in Chicago Heights. This was considered the Serena Hills area and was directly around the corner from Robert's parents. This area was the Homewood Flossmoor School district. Robert closed on the property, and the same day we pulled down orange flower wallpaper and painted the whole house before we moved in. I was still working at Landauer and our new house was only seven minutes away from my job. My husband was getting worse by the day and I had to work many hours to make ends meet. I would work from 8am-5pm and went back to work at night from 7pm-11pm. I did this a long time because Robert wasn't holding a job with his condition. It was getting so bad he was giving the car up for drugs. He did this several times and I finally told him if he didn't get my car, I was calling the police. One night, he slowly drove back into the driveway with the lights out as if I couldn't see him pulling the car in the driveway.

Robert had a brother that would come out periodically from the westside. They would utilize the upstairs family room. I had rehabbed from attic space. Our house was a Cape Cod design. One side of the property was a bedroom for the girls and the other side was unfinished. So, these guys would do their drugs and drink upstairs in that space and I would get on my bicycle and go for a ride almost every night. This was a way to free my mind and make it through another day.

I was working one day and received a call from my middle sister, Dellareesa and she told me she needed assistance with Michael. This news was a surprise to me as I listened. I was already overwhelmed and told her I would take Michael to give her a chance to get herself together. I reached out to our mother and explained what was going on with Della. Shortly afterwards my parents put Michael on the plane and I got Michael. He was two or three years old. He cried a lot because he missed his mother.

After a while, he got better. One day, I came home and Robert was sitting outside while he allowed June Bug to continuously spray water in Michaels face, to a point he couldn't catch his breath. They were playing a little too rough for me. Another day, I came home, and June Bug and Michael were playing in the dryer. Not to mention, one day Monique and Michael were playing, and Michael accidently hit Monique in the eye. When I got home, Robert had beat Michael so badly he had knots all over his head. I was very angry and told him I would report him to the Department of Children and Family services, and I did. He ran around to his parent's house and they had a meeting without me regarding what had happened. Robert came home and told me I had to get Michael out of his house. I called my parents and told them what happened, and I was trying to help Michael and he got badly hurt under my watch. My parents told me to send Michael back to them and they will help raise Michael. DCFS came out and had an initial interview and presented the consequences of what would happen if this happened again. I informed DCFS I was sending Michael back to Baltimore to be in my parent's care. I was very relieved that I didn't have to worry about Michael being abused anymore under my care.

Now Robert's brother from the west side got himself in a little trouble and Mac, Robert's older brother on his stepmother's side came out to the suburbs to visit us. Johnnie B got arrested, and Mac needed to get his car put in my name. I was so green and didn't understand everything happening, but I got the car and kept it in our garage. One night unexpectantly, Robert sent Melvin to get my car to bring him some gas, so I told Melvin I was going with him. I wasn't too keen on giving Melvin my keys, so I drove to the location where Robert was. Lord have mercy, this man had taken the BMW out of the garage and is out joy riding with another woman in the car with him. When he saw my car, he jumped out the BMW and put the gas in the car as fast as possible. When he saw me, Robert dropped that gas can and took off in the BMW. It was very foggy that night and you would think we were Starsky and Hutch while I was chasing him in the fog in my Buick. He had a woman in the car, and I was going to run him over. I was on his bumper about to pounce on him, when Robert made a turn, I lost him in the fog. I thank God for taking care of babies and fools, the old folk would say. I got married to be with one man and it seem like my husband was not of the same mindset. He continuously brought home Chlamydia. Dr. Watkins would always say, "Are you going to stay there until he kills you?"

The children were going to school and June Bug didn't want to go to school on Tuesday for some reason. He was also in love with Michael Jackson music. He had the Jacket and the curly hairdo to match. He took his curl spray to school every day and the teacher said he was always in the bathroom. This was not a good reason for him to not want to go to school, so I had to do a little investigating on my own and discovered the teacher was slapping him at school. Of course, I nipped this one in the bud right away and got resolution to the issue. In elementary school, June Bug was also checking out books from the library that high school children were reading, and the teacher had some concerns regarding that, but it all worked out. Tonya pretty much stuck to herself and read a lot of medical journals. There was only one problem with that. The girl was always diagnosing herself with something she read in those medical journals. Therefore, I had to take those books away from her. Tonya also kept herself as far away from her dad as possible. Robert would drive past the bus stop and kids would ask, who's dad is that and Tonya would reply, I don't know. Robert would have that crazy look on his face and Tonya never owned up to who he was. With Tonya being the oldest, I leaned on her to watch things while I worked at night. One day, I got a call that the house was on fire and when I got home to find out what happened, June Bug said a bird flew through the upstairs window and struck a match. Thank God Tonya put the fire out. With no bathroom upstairs she had to bring glasses of water upstairs to put out the fire.

God is so good, and I was eternally grateful that my children didn't get hurt. However, June Bug stabbed his sister in the leg with scissors because she told me he did it. He got his next shouting lesson that day.

CHAPTER 12

Hearing The Voice Of God

I rarely wore my jewelry to work because I worked on machinery and didn't want to damage my jewelry. One day, I checked my jewelry and went into my top drawer to look my jewelry over because my husband was stealing my credit cards and everything. To my surprise, Mr. Pryor had stolen my jewelry which included my wedding ring, my Class of 72 class ring, my amethyst ring and much more. Robert was selling my stuff for drugs and this was painful. When I mentioned to him my jewelry was missing, he helped me look for it in the house. He said, it must be here somewhere, Jan. Did you look over here, did you look over there? He was diligently looking for my jewelry himself when he knew all along, he sold my jewelry. I didn't know what to do, but I knew there was something seriously wrong with my husband. Me and the children had been through so much with him and were continuously trying to be supportive. It seemed to work for a while and then bam it happens again and again and again.

Monique was the baby and she just wandered around the house doing what she liked to do. One day, Monique broke out in bumps all over her body and when I called Dr. Watkins office, they told me not to bring her out because she had the measles. So, I kept her at home, and she got worse. She had a fever and her skin started peeling. She couldn't swallow or eat anything. God told me to keep her washed down in rubbing alcohol to break the fever and I did. I called the doctor's office back and Dr. Watkins had me bring her in right away because it sounded like she had scarlet fever and she did. Thank God for his divine protection again over my children.

Monique was watched by her father most of the time and she took advantage of the poor fellow when he was under the influence of alcohol. She had this plastic bat and used it occasionally to wake her father up out of his deep sleep. She would hit him in the head with her plastic bat. She also found my Shalimar cologne and sprayed him really good with it on another occasion. This is the best one right here, she found my makeup and gave her daddy the best makeup job a three-year-old could give. She used foundation, powder, blush, and red lip stick. Robert was outdone and couldn't believe he slept through all of that.

I was still in church believing my God would make away for me. My Pastor's oldest daughter was getting married and they asked me to help fry the chicken for the reception. It seemed like I fried chicken all day. I had my clothes already so when I finished frying chicken, I would go home and get dressed for the wedding. When I got home, I found someone had put paint all over my dress. My cologne was broken outside in the backyard and my wig was thrown outside. I was deeply hurt and this time I had really had enough. When Robert came home, he said he didn't do it and one day I will find out the truth. It didn't matter anymore. I snapped and lost my cotton-picking mind. I had been abused for over 10 years now. I worked hard trying to keep my family together because I was raised without my father and cried for my father constantly. I didn't want my kids to be without their father. That day, all those designer jeans I bought him and clothes he had, I cut off the legs of every pair of pants he had. I hung the pants on the wall so he could see them when he came back home. I'm sure the kids were so scared. They took all the knives and sharp objects and hid them in their room upstairs. I waited patiently for Robert to come home and he eventually did. When he entered the house, I guess he felt my rage and yelled upstairs to the kids and told them you all can go to bed, because it will not be a fight tonight. When he entered the bedroom and saw his jeans cut up and hanging on the wall, he didn't say a word. Robert was a very revengeful man and I knew this and should have been prepared for it.

One day, I took out a pair of shoes and they were cut up. Dummy me, I should have checked all my shoes that day, but got another surprise when I went to get another pair of shoes. I collected shoes and man, this was painful to see he got me back by cutting up all my shoes and never said a word. I guess crime never pays. We were still attending family counseling. When the therapist started asking questions about what was going on in the house, the children never said a word. We also had family sessions at home on Wednesday nights so the kids could talk to us about anything with no retaliation from the parents. One evening in one of our discussions, the children looked at me and asked me why don't I get them out of this family problem. After all, I was the one who was saved, so I should do something to make life better for them. This hit me like a ton of bricks because I considered myself as the good parent and my children were angry with me for not getting them out of this horrible living condition. Unbeknown to them I had actually filed for a divorce, but Robert didn't acknowledge the paperwork and I didn't have all the money for the final payment. This caused my case to be closed.

One evening while Robert and I were lying in the bed, he asked me what happened to the baby and I told him my mother made me go to New York to have an abortion. He started screaming, I knew it, I knew it. That's why I have been treating you like this for the past 10 years, to make you pay for what you had done. I looked at him with tears in my eyes remembering how I cried out to God to please forgive me for such a horrible act because I didn't believe in abortion. I told him, "You mean God has forgiven me but you haven't. This is unreal." Then he made a statement that the hunter got captured by the prey. He never loved me initially, he only married me to get me pregnant and leave me. Still, he eventually fell in love with me but continued to be very abusive.

I went to church one Sunday after that conversation and a gentleman, I called my brother who was from Ghana said, "I don't know what's wrong with you American women, why are you paying the mortgage, when that's your husband's responsibility. Stop paying the mortgage." Well, I thought about what he had said and went home and reasoned with myself. Robert was actually always telling me to get out of his house so it might be time for me to do just that. Therefore, I filed a second time for a divorce and I stopped paying the mortgage on the house. One day, I came home and there was a red sticker on the door. I guess Robert never paid no attention to the notices he was receiving regarding his house. I had concern now though; I didn't want the kids to come home and see our furniture was put out on the curb.

So now, I needed to find a place for us to stay. One preacher from Memphis was here preaching in Kankakee and Robert and I went every night to Revival. I pressed my way because I was still trying to find answers to my problems. How do you get a better marriage? We were standing around the alter one night and Deacon Willie Finch mentioned to Robert he had some property in the Heights and needed to get someone in there. Every time he fixed it up, someone would break in and steal the house supplies. Robert immediately told Deacon Finch, Janice needs a place to stay and the rest was history. If I had not pressed my way to Revival every night driving to Kankakee, I may have missed my opportunity to receive my blessing that God had for me. I moved my family out of the house on Fredrick Drive and it seemed like we stepped backwards when we moved to the east side of Chicago Heights.

However, we needed a place to stay and I wasn't too proud to move back to the east side of the Heights. The property was vacant and there hadn't been any maintenance regarding bugs. We had to fight roaches every night until we could get them under control because they were crawling everywhere. Robert and I stayed up most of the night killing these bugs. We gave the children the bedrooms and we set our bed up in the living room. I couldn't sleep at night because the neighbors stayed up all night selling drugs and sleeping all day when I had to be up for work. My husband was still on drugs and everywhere I moved, he moved with me. I got ready to go to work one morning and the Holy Spirit told me to check the gas tank. So, I didn't start the car but walked around the car checking for what I could find and discovered that Mr. Pryor had put syrup in the gas tank. I walked from Lowe Avenue in Chicago Heights to Glenwood, Illinois to get to work.

After I arrived at work, I called the police to report that my husband had put syrup in the gas tank of our car. I still had the yellow Buick and when I got home that night, Henry Rice made him take the gas tank off and clean it out. Robert made sure he showed me that he cleaned the gas tank. Robert was very smart and could do anything he wanted to when he put his mind to it. Since he was acting out very badly, I got a steering wheel jack so he couldn't take the car anymore. Well, Mr. Pryor showed me who was boss. He took the tire off the car, removed the brake shoes and pads which released the breaks. Then he was able to remove the steering wheel jack off the car. He told me I better not ever try to lock the car from him again. I couldn't believe this dude. I was still praying to my God, "I'm here and I don't have anyone to turn to for help Lord, I need help." One-night Tonya screamed and cried and said something was in her ear and Robert took her to the hospital and they found a roach in her ear. She also took some pills and tried to take her life. We were all going through so much. This was very heavy on my heart. I have never heard of anyone trying to take their life and I may not have handled every issue correctly. I did the best I could, while going through all these traumatic situations almost every day.

One afternoon, while trying to chill in the apartment, I heard a bunch of kids making a lot of noise and when I looked out the window, they had a kitten across the street. My first instinct was that they were playing with the kitten. They were on top of the garage across the street and were going to throw the kitten off the roof of the garage with a firecracker up the kitten's behind. I don't care too much for cats, but I would not let those kids kill that kitten. We rescued the kitten and it became Tonya's pet. Tonya was very fond of the kitten and named her Simba. I think Simba was good therapy for Tonya.

One Friday evening, I came home from work and I was very tired. Robert was in a weird mood. He was high off of something and drunk all at the same time. His mouth was twitching, his eyes were glossy, and he was very restless. I was lying down on the couch trying to wind down after a long day at work and he wouldn't let me sleep. He kept playing all these love songs and he continued to put the radio next to my head on the couch. I explained to him I was very tired and didn't understand why he wouldn't let me take a nap. He wouldn't stop playing the music in my ear, so I stopped asking him. He would look at me with those eyes of his and I couldn't figure out what was wrong that night. All of a sudden, I heard the Holy Ghost in a loud voice that said, "GET UP AND GET OUT NOW." I jumped up, grabbed my kids and the microwave, and we hurriedly left the house that night. Why the microwave you ask? It cost over $400 at that time and I didn't want Robert to sell it for drugs. I drove all around that night looking for a Hotel or Motel, but there wasn't a vacancy anywhere. So, I had to come all the way back to the Chicago Heights Holiday Inn located on Dixie Highway. I feared for my life because I thought whatever drunken or high state he was in that he would hurt me and my children. Also, because the hotel was close to the apartment I was sure he would find us. I didn't sleep well that night, watching over my children and looking out the window making sure Robert wasn't anywhere to be found.

The next morning, I had to check out of the Hotel and wondered if it was safe for me and the kids to return back to the apartment. After a while, we did go back to the apartment and it was business as usual. He remembered nothing that happened the night before, or he acted as if he didn't remember. Sometime later, his cousin who lived downstairs from us told me that my husband was plotting to heat up an iron and put it to my face that night. So, I am again eternally grateful that God told me to get out of that apartment and I am so glad I was obedient to the instructions of the Holy Ghost. If it wasn't for the Lord on my side where would I be? I am so thankful to the Lord for taking care of me in my time of trouble. He is a God that never sleeps nor slumbers. Amen and thank you Jesus for keeping your eyes on me and my family.

CHAPTER 13

On Time God

At work, the employees complained that they needed their money in their bank account and didn't want the Profit Sharing anymore. Unbeknown to me, one day I received 24k dollars in the mail and that was a Godsend. Truly, when you are trying to figure it out God has already worked it out. Sometimes when you think you are alone and feel like no one cares, let me tell you God cares for you. We were still living in that small apartment on the east side of Chicago Heights, and I was ready to move into my own house. Finally, I would have a home that I could call my own. During this time, my divorce was going through but Robert didn't respond to the summons. I spent some of the money fixing up the yellow Buick for Robert, and I took the family on a nice vacation touring the east coast in the new gray Buick I purchased for myself. We went to Baltimore first, which is where my parents were. I not only ate all the crabs I wanted; I cleaned my mother's house from top to bottom.

Sometimes I would make myself sick trying to do everything she needed before returning back home to Chicago. Next stop was Virginia to see Robert's cousins. As soon as we got out of the car in Saluda, Virginia, ticks grabbed our legs, feet, and ankles. Kathy, Robert's cousin, had to use matches to get the ticks out of our skin. Even though, Robert and I were going through, we made the best of our road trip and I think we enjoyed that trip. When driving to Baltimore and driving back to Chicago, we always stopped in Breezewood as a regular stop. We would get ice cream, food, gas, and souvenirs. Driving through the mountains and going through the tunnel while making our little pit stops along the way were always very pleasant. We would eat at every stop. What a beautiful drive this was.

When we returned home from our vacation, it was time to look for a house. I was eternally thankful to Deacon Willie Finch for renting his property to us, but it was time to get my own house. The Lord had blessed me right in time. I know you remembered me saying I had fixed up the yellow Buick. Well, we woke up to the alarming news that the yellow Buick was on fire.

Someone had set the car on fire. This was terrible because I had just spent a lot of money fixing the car up. Who would do a thing like that? I know what you a thinking. Robert did it right? Well, I'm really not sure whether he did it or not. He may not have wanted me to have my independence and wanted to limit us down to one car. However, it could have been the drug dealer. Who knows, I was glad no one got hurt when that car caught on fire.

I had contacted a real estate agent and looked for my house. I was trying to initially bid for a HUD house, but I was always the second highest bidder. I looked at houses in Robbins and Chicago Heights. I told the agent he was trying to show me houses that I didn't want and always in the neighbor-hoods I didn't want to move to. I needed to be close to my job and I wouldn't be able to handle a house with too many repairs. After a while, I realized it was time for me to get me a new agent. Her name was Priscilla Ball. This was the best decision I could have made. Priscilla showed me three houses and I needed to do a simple assumption, where no credit check was needed. You only needed to validate that you had the money in the bank, and you could assume the mortgage. My requirement was three bedrooms, two bathrooms, a garage and no basement. The last house we looked at located in University Park, Illinois was the house for me. When we were driving down the street, I noticed huge shadows of the houses casting in the street, and the leaves were dancing in the street moving back and forward as we drove to the property. I was thinking, these are some big houses in this village. When we arrived up to the property's driveway, this house was the smallest house on the whole block. When we entered the house, there was the smell of cleaning products and the house smelled nice. I walked in the house and checked out everything and absolutely fell in love with the kitchen. All our previous kitchens were ally way kitchens with very little room to maneuver in when preparing your meals. I was sold.

I was scheduled to close on December 1, 1988. The owners actually gave me the keys to the property before I closed on the house. Robert and I immediately came over to pull the carpet up because it was dirty. Guess what, when we opened the door to the house there was the strongest smell of cat urine I had ever smelled. That's why they were there with cleaning products to cover the smell of the cat urine. We consulted my agent and she told us to pull up the carpet, scrub the floors, let them dry and after they dry, paint all the floors. We did what we were instructed to do and the smell was gone.

One evening I received a knock on the door, and it was the neighbor behind me. They brought me cookies to welcome me into the neighborhood. A nice white lady with her daughter. The cookies were great, and it was nice of her to do that. A few days later, my Pastor's daughter came by to see the house and it wasn't in the shape I wanted it in, but I let her walk through anyway. She also welcomed me in the neighborhood.

You are probably wondering why Mr. Pryor is still hanging around. He is the only man I know that gets divorced and never moves out the house. Well, he wasn't exactly easy to get rid of either and once we got settled, Mr. Pryor was back at it. He was pawning the printers and whatever he could get his hands on. He was now doing crack cocaine and that was a doozy. When Robert did crack cocaine, he would be in the bed for three days at a time. I would bring him a face towel to wash his face and bring him breakfast in bed. There was a very distinct smell that came from his body from using crack cocaine. I could usually tell who was using crack by that smell. Robert was the father of my children and the word of God said in 1 Corinthians 7:14 the unbelieving husband is sanctified by the wife. Therefore, I continued taking care of him.

This went on for a long time and all seemed hopeless. I desperately wanted my husband clean from drugs and alcohol. When he was sober, he was the nicest man ever. He was very smart and could fix anything. Robert would give you the shirt off his back, but when he was bad, he was bad. Legislators determined that alcoholics and drug users were classified as having a disability and could qualify for SSDI. He was now receiving SSDI and had a little money to manage. Robert attended several programs to get clean and after going through another AAA support program for alcohol and drugs at Ingalls Hospital, he was sober for two years. We had the time of our lives. We did everything together. We cleaned the house, cut the grass, and cooked together. I supported him at every AAA meeting and substance abuse counseling. He would be in his session and I would either sit in the car reading a book or stay in the waiting room until he finished his session when there wasn't a class for me. I would bring something to do, because I wanted to show my support.

CHAPTER 14

Sobriety

Things were looking good for Robert for a minute. He was back in church and helping out in the ministry. He had even approached the Pastor to see if he could start an AAA program at the Facility. However, he was turned down, and this was very disappointing to Robert. He continued with his support group despite of the disappointment. So, how many of you know misery loves company? Your partners in crime will come looking for you when you are trying to better yourself. One of Robert's cousins came by the house in a new car. Robert had been clean for two years, and he had a job at the railroad. Things were looking up for our family. When Robert returned home from his little joy ride his mouth was twitching, his eyes were glossy, and he was crying and asking me to pray for him. I prayed for him while he was in the car and it was hard for Robert to gain that leverage again towards sobriety. He said he was sorry and didn't mean to do it. The cousin was gone home, and our family was set back two years. When you are trying to change your life it's important to change your people, places, and things. It's important that you wait until you are strong enough to handle being around friends that are still doing the very thing you are trying to stop. Sometimes friends will do anything to get you back out there. You must fill your heart and mind with the word of God and be determined not to tempt yourself. Identify a support contact person you can call when struggling with temptation.

It was getting bad around the house. June Bug and Tonya were in high school now and June Bug had a friend that got burned out and the boy's mother wanted to know if they could stay with me for a while. Well, the mom stayed a few days and left her son with me. I wasn't going to put the child out, so I kept him so he could finish high school. Gangs were trying to recruit my son and every night when we went to bed, they were throwing things at our window and then running away. It got to the point that I began driving my son to school and picking him up because of gang activity in the neighborhood. On Robert Jr's birthday, we gave him a barbeque and he had so many boys in the house we couldn't move. I told them it was too many and they had to go outside. Well guess who else went outside. Yep, you are right. Robert went outside with all the boys, turned his hat to the side, pimped across the street with his hands swinging behind him. He had his stick in his hand, still pimping around the cars parked outside. June Bug asked his dad nicely if he would go back in the house and Robert got very angry at June Bug. He went straight crazy that night. He also had a metal mallet in his hand and threw it at our son. I am thankful to God he didn't hit June Bug with that mallet because the way it hit the house; he would have killed our son that night. The party was over.

June Bugs party was ruined and I was also fed up with every holiday being ruined because Robert was passed out in the bed from his festivities from the night before with the fellows. By the time he got up on the holiday, the day was almost over.

This holiday would be my last holiday ruined because of drugs and alcohol. I went outside and found the charcoal and lighter fluid. I washed and seasoned my meat, started that grill and I have been grilling ever since that holiday. When Mr. Pryor woke up, we had eaten and wiped our mouths.

Robert also had a bad habit of starting arguments when he wanted to do drugs. I told him to keep the argument and go do what you do. No one wants to fight all the time. You are grown. Go get your drugs, you don't need to create an excuse to do it. Stop trying to justify your actions based on an argument you started in the first place.

I was still attending church every Sunday singing in the choir, helping senior citizens, supporting the ministry, and getting my praise on. When I go to church, I try to look like everything is just fine. I have on my Sunday's best. I love people so it was easy for me to keep smiling and giving my hugs each week. Church was an escape from the troubles I was going through at home. The seniors at the church kept me busy frying chicken and raising money for special efforts. Sometimes things got hard for me. Robert paid no attention to his mother, sister, or brother for that matter. He had a mind of his own. There were days I wanted to get down in a corner and scream, but I would think on something good and something positive. I would praise God for the little things and before you know it, you begin to feel just fine. Sometimes you must encourage yourself.

One night, he was supposed to meet me back at the church when choir rehearsal was over, and I waited and waited. Robert never showed up, so I had to leave him. The men at the church would not leave me there by myself. Therefore, I drove home. After getting in bed and practically falling asleep, the Holy Ghost told me to go back and pick Robert up. So, I resisted a little but knew I needed to get up and go get Robert. When I found him, he was walking on Western Ave, just passing the U-Haul business. He was happy to see me and said thank you Jan, thank you Jan for coming to get me. It was pitch black outside and I got up because of God's' instructions. I am glad I was obedient to the Holy Spirit.

Because of what the family was going through, Tonya acted out and wanted to live her own life. Monique was trying to figure out what was wrong with her daddy and throwing up every time he started an argument and Rob was trying to be the man of the house. It got so bad that I asked Robert one Sunday morning, if I could anoint and pray for him. He told me I couldn't save him. I told the Devil I wasn't talking to him and I wanted to speak to Robert. I called Robert's name and asked him if I could anoint and pray with him that morning and he didn't open his mouth. After no response, I told him when I get back from church if he wasn't out of here, I know someone bigger and stronger than him that was going to get him out. When I got back from church Robert was packed up and his brother from Chicago was there to pick him up. Now, generally I would let the rascal come back after a few weeks, but this time, I promised God I would not let him back home unless God brought him back.

He called me and stated he had never been away from home this long. I told him I couldn't handle it anymore and he needed to get his own place. Now, he never stopped trying to figure out how to get back home. He told me he slept with his bible every night under his pillow. He told me he had a dream and his bed was on fire, and it must be the Lord trying to tell him something. Nothing moved me this time. I had been disappointed so often with his salvation stories, that I didn't believe him anymore.

Robert didn't stay on the west side long, so I helped him get an apartment with the Housing Authority for Seniors and Veterans in Chicago Heights. He only stayed there for a little while because he didn't follow the rules of the Housing Authority, so they canceled his lease.

CHAPTER 15

To See My Father

Robert was working at the Salvation Army in Chicago Heights. Through that organization, Robert was given an opportunity to move to Kansas City to participate in their program. Robert had to stay in that program for one year to complete the program. While Robert was in that program, he was also volunteering at the Salvation Army, and he constantly sent me things that he thought I liked. He was always writing me letters and sharing his feelings with me in the letters. He eventually realized what we could have had together as a couple, if he would have gotten himself together. One day, I received a call from Robert, and he said some woman he was in relations with was shooting at his car and he needed to get out of town. He didn't have enough money to make it to Louisville, Kentucky where his sister lived.

He needed me to wire him money to St. Louis so he could make it to Louisville. I remember thinking to myself there aren't too many Janice Pryor's out there. No one will put up with his behavior. He told me that day on the phone I was his only friend and thank you for wiring me the money. He said he had no one else to turn to.

Robert was now living with his sister in Louisville, Kentucky and he landed a job at the Marriott as one of the cooks. He met another young lady that lived in the projects and tried to have a relationship with her. One day, he called me at work and told me now he knows how I felt trying to have something with someone who didn't want anything. This young lady had a little girl and Robert spoiled her. He loved to eat so he made sure everybody got fed. Robert traveled home to Chicago Heights and brought his girlfriend back with him. He fired up the grill and cooked, which was something he enjoyed doing. We all finished our meal and Robert wanted to show his girlfriend off to Uncle Buck, who lived around the corner from me. He told Uncle Buck I was around there feeding his women. Now, I am a nice person and always try to do the right thing, but I was as mad as two Billy goats butting heads. Robert was over visiting his children and decided to cook out. I was raised to do unto others as you would have them do unto you. I was trying to be hospitable. When Uncle Buck told me what Robert said, I told myself there will never be another meal coming from me. No siree, not at all. The next day was Sunday and my children and I were getting ready for church. Robert called me and said Jan, my friend wants to catch a ride to church with you this morning, is that all right? Well, I was still burning from the comments he told the neighbor and I told Robert there were two cars around there where he was and if he wanted her to get a ride to church, he better get up and take her to church himself. I had reached my limit.

Robert went back to Louisville. After a while, Monique was whining about wanting her daddy. She missed her daddy and made a song whining for him. She was crying so much for her daddy. I told her she could go and stay with him on spring break. Off to Louisville she went. While she was down there the lady was cursing her out and one day Monique didn't get out of bed until her daddy got back home. She said to that lady, my momma doesn't curse at me and you aren't either. While Monique was in Louisville, she asked her dad if she could get a tattoo and I agreed for her to get a small one. Now, use your imagination and tell me if you guessed what she got on her leg. Yes, it was a big huge, gigantic rose covering her leg. I was very disappointed, but the damage was already done.

Spring break was over now and when Monique got back home, the first thing out of her mouth was I don't know how you stayed with that man all these years. That was her last visit.

Robert had siblings on the westside of Chicago which included a set of twins, Kristine and Karla. One evening Karla went out with her boyfriend against her better judgement and on the way home they were involved in a car accident. They were hit by a drunk driver. The impact was so bad that Karla was killed in that accident. This was terrible news. Robert and his sister Delores lived in Louisville and came home for the funeral. When I spoke to Robert on the phone, I asked him how he was doing, and his reply was he was doing good, but he couldn't control his saliva. I told him after the funeral was over, I needed to take him to the hospital. Robert went to the westside and stayed with his siblings for a while and they said he just laid down and wasn't very mobile or talkative at all. When he got back south that night it was too late to go all the way to VA Hines Hospital, so I told him when he got back home, he needed to go to the hospital right away. I made him promise me because he never wanted to go to the doctor unless it was absolutely necessary. I had to go to work the next day and they were leaving for Louisville. Around noon, I got a call from Robert and he told me he would not make it all the way back to Louisville. So, I told him when I get off work, I would take him to the hospital.

When we arrived at the hospital it was a long wait, but when they triaged Robert, they discovered he had already had a heart attack and stroke. They admitted him right away. I stayed until they got him in a room, calmed down and situated for the night. This man was the father of my children and I was supportive for my children. I went to the hospital every night, driving from University Park to VA Hines Hospital on 1st Ave in Chicago. While Robert was in the hospital, he had another stroke and they needed to take him down for tests. Robert couldn't talk but I could see he was very scared, so I stayed with him during the test. I could tell by looking in his eyes he had a deep concern about what was happening to him. Robert came up for his sister's funeral and was hospitalized immediately afterwards. Delores, his oldest sister returned to Louisville alone. His girlfriend was home in Louisville Kentucky who did not attend the funeral. After a few days, they thought he had HIV Aids because nothing was working, but they ruled that out. One day I asked the kids, to go with me to the hospital to visit their dad and nobody wanted to go with me. I received a call from the Hospital later that day and Robert had fallen out of the bed. They thought he had a seizure. After receiving that news, everyone was ready to go with me to the hospital. After we arrived, they had put him in restraints because his body was jerking uncontrollably.

They had to sedate him to keep him calm. He could only make noises with his mouth and couldn't talk at all anymore.

Robert had been in the hospital nearly three weeks now. With Tonya being pregnant and being on total bedrest, Monique rode to the hospital with me. When we arrived in his room, he was still heavily sedated and there was no motion, so Monique and I sang a song to him. While we were singing to Robert as he lay there lifeless with no sign of movement, there came a tear running down his face. I told Monique, he can hear us singing to him, but that was the only sign of life we saw that night; the tear running down his cheek.

The children were the next of kin and the hospital was trying to get them to remove the life support, which was very difficult for the children to do. How do you say take away the oxygen and food and let him die? The children couldn't make that decision, so I fell on my knees and pleaded with God, for him to not allow the children to have to make this decision regarding their father's life. I prayed to the Lord and asked Him to let his will be done because I knew those kids would not unhook their father. One night shortly afterwards in the early morning, we got the call that Robert's organs had shut down and had passed away that night. We loaded up and went to the hospital to view the body. While we were in the room, they asked the children if they needed a Chaplain and the children almost in unison said our mom is a minister. We joined hands and we prayed over Robert's body that night. I remembered when we were at his sister's funeral not even a month ago, Robert had a Holy Ghost good time praising God. He had his own Amen corner in that church and he wasn't ashamed to let anyone know he knew and loved the Lord. He was standing up and opening his mouth and bellowing out praise unto the Lord. Robert said nothing in church. When he went to court and the Judge asked him if he had anything to say, Robert never opened his mouth, but this day he had a praise on his lips. He had a different look about him. I was thinking to myself is this the same man, because this time I can see a change in him. Robert was never one to be a hypocrite. If he wasn't right, he didn't want to go in the church house. I just sat there and watched Robert Charles Pryor Sr. get his praise on. If I can use my sanctified mind, I was thinking that the Lord knew my husband's struggles and he knew the pain he endured with his addiction.

Robert never gave up trying to get clean from drugs. He said he was going to beat this thing. He told me it took 10 tries for anything to happen when he tried cocaine. I told him God was trying to tell you something. The Lord doesn't make a mistake, and God took him home on a high note. He was delivered and healed on the other side. Robert never made it back to Kentucky, he was funeralized in Glenwood, IL. His mother wouldn't let the children bury him in the VA Cemetery, so they bought a plot in Glenwood Cemetery. I'm looking back and remembering how he enrolled into the military on a buddy buddy plan with his cousins. He was the only one that passed the test. The funny thing about it was, he said he just checked anything on the test.

Tonya delivered her baby one week after his death and was very sad that he would never get to see his beautiful granddaughter, London Paighe Brooks. Monique talked to her dad alone in her room. Rob just bottled everything up inside of him. Monique finished college and we all went on about our lives. I am so thankful to the Lord for keeping his hands on me and my family through the ordeals we had to endure in life because my husband was a sick man. He returned home from the military a sick man and couldn't get him the help he needed because I didn't have Robert's consent. I'm sure I am not the only spouse of a veteran that endured a lot of abuse because your veteran spouse was mentally disabled due to going through so much while protecting our country.

While I was going through all the drama, my Lord and Savior kept me and my children safe in his arms. I couldn't see God when I was going through sometimes, but I never left God or my church. The church was my place of refuge.

I am so glad I know God the Father, God the Son, and God the Holy Ghost. Veterans, if you feel you need support, stop explaining it away. Go get the help you need to sustain a certain quality of life. I salute all the veterans. God Bless and keep you. To all the spouses of Veterans, stay strong and keep the Lord in your life. Remember you are never alone.

Behind the Scenes Scriptures

1 Corinthians 7:14

For the unbelieving husband is sanctified by the wife, and the unbelieving wife is sanctified by the husband: else were your children unclean, but now are they holy

1Corinthians 10:13

There hath no temptation taken you but such as is common to man: but God is faithful, who will not suffer you to be tempted above that ye are able; but will with temptation also make a way to escape, that ye may be able to bear it.

James 5:13

Is any among you afflicted? Let him pray, is any merry? let him sing psalms

Mathew 6:33

But seek ye first the kingdom of God, and his righteousness; and all these things shall be added unto you.

Behind the Scenes Scriptures

Mathew 7:13

Enter ye in at the strait gate, and broad is the way, that leadeth to destruction, and many there be which go in thereat.

Philippians 4:13

I can do all things through Christ which strengtheneth me

Psalms 23:1

The Lord is my shepherd; I shall not want

Psalms 113.3

From the rising of the sun unto the going down of the same the Lords name is to be praised.

Romans 8:1

There is therefore now no condemnation to them which are in Christ Jesus, who walk not after the flesh, but after the Spirit

Romans 8:28

And we know all things work together for the good of them that love God, to them who are the called according to his purpose.

VA Referrals

SAMHSA – Substance Abuse and Mental Heath Services Administration

National Helpline – 1-800-662-4357

Website: https://www.samhsa.gov/find-help/national-helpline

PTSD and Substance Abuse in Veterans

Veterans Crisis Line – 1-800-273-8255

Website: https://www.ptsd.va.gov

Thank You

CKJ PUBLISHING

and

DML EDITING & WRITING
GYPECC

Dominique Lambright, Owner/Editor/Writer

DML Editing & Writing

Dmleditingandwriting.com

262-939-7929